WORDS IN HARMONY

Edited by

Heather Killingray

First published in Great Britain in 2000 by
POETRY NOW
Remus House,
Coltsfoot Drive,
Woodston,
Peterborough, PE2 9JX
Telephone (01733) 898101
Fax (01733) 313524

All Rights Reserved

Copyright Contributors 2000

HB ISBN 0 75430 957 6
SB ISBN 0 75430 958 4

Foreword

Although we are a nation of poets we are accused of not reading poetry, or buying poetry books. After many years of listening to the incessant gripes of poetry publishers, I can only assume that the books they publish, in general, are books that most people do not want to read.

Poetry should not be obscure, introverted, and as cryptic as a crossword puzzle: it is the poet's duty to reach out and embrace the world.

The world owes the poet nothing and we should not be expected to dig and delve into a rambling discourse searching for some inner meaning.

The reason we write poetry (and almost all of us do) is because we want to communicate: an ideal; an idea; or a specific feeling. Poetry is as essential in communication, as a letter; a radio; a telephone, and the main criterion for selecting the poems in this anthology is very simple: they communicate.

CONTENTS

The Natural World	Parivash Jeelani	1
Pollution	Greeny 2000	2
A Precious Place	Vicky McHugh	3
Mood Swings In Nature	Angus Richmond	4
Anything Pure	Clare Newsome	5
Years Of Hurt	Robert Dickins	6
Please Listen To Me	Kayleigh Hardy	7
Gone But Not Forgotten	Colin Allsop	8
An Ugly Place	Rebecca Butler	9
Beauty And The Beast	Peter Webb	10
Seeing The Unseen	Hannah Cummins	12
Unfriendly Man	J Blades	13
Un Shore	Amy Phillips	14
Weeds	Terry Flower	15
Sexes On The Beach...	Lucy Burgan	16
Girls On Boys	Daniela Hardy	17
The First Days Of Being Single	Erin Halliday	18
Soulmate	Elizabeth Myra Crellin	19
The Truth Always Comes Through	Sheralee Le-Gros	20
Waterfall Of Tears	Charlotte Cook	21
The Dream Train	Elaine Walklet	22
Blue	Sara Harris	23
Spurned Lover	A Branthwaite	24
He Was Born Today	Ann Hathaway	25
Deepest, Darkest Fathoms	Patricia Cunningham	26
A Walk In The Woods	Wendy Dawson	27
Dream On	Roger S Foster	28
Hypothesising	B M Hurll	29
School Days	G G Swepstone	30
A Hero's Farewell	Emmanuel Petrakis	31
Clinging Elian	Hilary Jill Robson	32
The New Postman	Katherine Fell	34
Only A Name?	Ann Beard	35
Perhaps I'll Write A Poem	Terry Daley	36

Time To Shoo!	Tom Ritchie	37
Second World War . . .	Joyce Hemsley	38
Our World Today	E K Jones	40
My Greatest Loss	Martin Selwood	41
A Walk On The Wild Side	Hazel Cooper	42
The ABC Of My Love For Chocolate	Jean Wearn Wallace	43
A Say On Words	N Lemel	44
The Kiss	Jean Paisley	45
None But You	Lee Grace	46
Unforgotten Sacrifice	Michael Smith	47
A Heart Of Gold, A Life Of Sin	Donna Marie Hardie	48
Our Plight	Saheeda Khan	49
A Has-Been Madam	John Taylor	50
Final Darkness	Helen Riley	51
Chant	Athol Cowen	52
The Marriage	G Clarke	53
Red Rose (Of Life)	Jiwamalar Perumal	54
Retribution	Knolly La Fortune	55
Picture On The Wall	T Lawrence	56
Space Lies	Lachlan Taylor	57
The Post	Julia Murphy	58
Shadow Man	S M Thompson	59
Live A Holy Life	Richard Clewlow	60
Whose House?	Susan Sutherland	61
How *Stoopid* Can Men Get?	Barbara Sherlow	62
A Toast To British Pubs	Kopan Mahadeva	63
I Held Spring In My Hand	Emma-Louise Cartwright	64
Degeneration Gap	Phoenix Martin	65
Insomnia	Stacey Quimby	66
Cohen's Song	Rod Trott	67
The Autumn Tankard	Roy Millar	68
Rainbows	Peter Huggins	69
Cloned	V B D'Wit	70
Onward To 2000	Andrew Sutherland	71
Sea Of Daffodils	Joan Strong	72
The Tunnel Of Love	Ken Gilbert	73

Title	Author	Page
The Golden Years	Bert Booley	74
Maltese Magic	Paul Harvey Jackson	75
Springtime	M Muirhead	76
No Identity	Joyce	77
The Ceremony	J G Ryder	78
Knowledge v Wisdom	Robert A Hardwidge	80
Reflections On Perfection	Les D Pearce	81
My Grandma's Last Goodbye	Frances Gibson	82
Pearly Dawn	Evelyn Balmain	83
Just Passing By	Jenny Anderson	84
Look At You	Judi B	85
Growing Up	Frank E Trickett	86
Walk Upon Better Bridges	Debbie Perks	87
Memories Forever	Jeanette Gaffney	88
Keeping Away From Danger	Jan McCaffery	89
Endless Journey	M J Bull	90
Reach Your Goal	Denise Shaw	91
The Greatest Gift	Mary Hudson	92
Kath - The Little Lady Who Cared	Jan Graver-Wild	93
Journey Of The Dying	Kathleen Farrell	94
Red Blues	John Smurthwaite	95
Prisoner Of Love	Jennifer Abdulazeez	96
Ice Maiden	Kim Montia	97
Dreamtime	Stephen Gyles	98
'Vacancies Pour Tous' In France	Gillian C Fisher	99
Child Of Life	Rowland Warambwa	100
The Best Things In Life Are Free	Brenda Irene Piper	101
A Perfect Day	S J Davidson	102
When The Ice Melts	Jennifer Dunkley	103
Ancient Habitat	Jeremy Jones	104
Awakening Call	Olive Bedford	106
Spanish Orange	Anna Moore	107
See The Point?	John L Wright	108
Wishes	Carol Olson	109
Strange Jury!	A Goodwin	110

Complicated	Hannah Shooter	111
Secret Thoughts	Diana Daley	112
Mother	M Kelly	113
Silver Moon	Eileen Coleman	114
Milly's Mayhem	Nikky Ingram	115
A Wishing Well	Anthony Manville	116
What A Surprise	Anne McTavish	118
Uncompetitive Man	T A Napper	119
The Stranger	Barbara Rose Ling	120
Saturn Swimming	Daryl Gilham	121
Robin And His Men Of Green	Colin Farmer	122
Changing Rooms	Ann G Wallace	124
Frog In The Throat	B G Clarke	126
Magnolia Lament	Pat Holton	127
A Poet's Fareweill Tae Ye Bonnie Lass	Gilbert	128
Snap	Lola Perks-Hartnell	129
The Magic Shoe	Margaret T Emmerson	130
Rainbow	Edward Fursdon	132
Sheherezade	Denise Marriott	133
Night Fear	Vara Humphreys	134
Lament From The Aquarium	J M Service	135
Faction Fighters	Gary J Finlay	136
Facts Or Fiction 2000	Brian Marshall	137
Love In The Forest	F Hirst	138
Escape	David Brownley	140
When The Wind Blows	Linda Zulaica	141
The Story Of My Life!	John Tirebuck	142
Nature's Curse	H W Fleming	144
The Testimonial Match	Roger Carpenter	145
Summer Idyll	G D C Stribling	146
Liza Jane	Ria Telford	147
Work Experience	June Slater	148
The Spirits Danced At Midnight	Faith Honeysett	149
Instinct Of A Pet Collie Dog	Elizabeth Wynne	150
Dandy Jack The Highwayman	Bardon	151
The Last Of His Kind	Bronwyn Lewis	152

Pretenders	Stephen Atkinson	154
Sea Dog's Seed Bed	Frederick Poole	155
Stars And Spikes	Penwork 2000	156
Deserted Friend	Geraldine Bruce	157
An Age Of Gold	Anita Richards	158
Young MacDonald's Farm	Margaret Richer	159
Shadows Of The Night	V C Gregory	160
A Knight In A Raincoat	Margaret Connolly	161
Running The Gauntlet	Ivy Cawood	162
The Duel	Carole Hoy	163
Sam	Mandy Craven	164
The Old Bucket	Haidee Williams	165
The Lighthouse	Norman Mason	166
Child Of Mine And Child Of Yours	Wynne Stearns	167
Picking Up The Pieces	Donna Marie Smart	168
Mick's Story	Betsy Van Warmer	169
Magical Mystery Tour	J Freeborough	170
Memory Lane	Frederick Coles	171
Second-Hand Heroes	D Adams	172
The Explosion	Debra Becker	173
Soldier Toy	Sarah Horton	174
The Match	Anne R Cooper	175
Sharon	Paul Wilkins	176
Tiger, Tiger Burning Bright	Bill Hayles	177
Our Back Doorstep	Glenn Granter	178
Charlie	D Riches	179
Silently	Maureen Arnold	180
Love In The Afternoon	Bonita Hall	181
Through The Trees	John Costin	182
My Pet	Sonia Bowen	183
To A Granddaughter And Her Child	Maureen Lindsey	184
Cats By Night	Ann Copland	185
Killing Fields	Dorrien Thomas	186
My Journey	J Steggles	187

THE NATURAL WORLD

A s time flies past, humans grow blinder,
B odies start demolishing lands.
C reatures lose homes, run far away,
D art into extinction's hands.
E very day more and more forests destroyed,
F lames and machines are used.
G olden of sunshine, now black as ebony,
H erds of animals abused.
I n the air, or smoke in some,
J oy is absorbed and jailed in.
K illed are the spirits of so many others,
L ost ones mourned from within.
M onkeys hang on, but not from the trees,
N o, for their life, but still,
O bserve their situation, know won't survive,
P erish soon they will.
Q uestion is retreat, answer is no,
R ealise humans do not.
S oon all the birds, lions and snakes
T oo shall be gone, the lot.
U nder the branches, lay all the dying,
V ultures circling see red,
W ill the world ever see those again?
X tremely rare were the dead.
Y et, people act alike,
Z ombies at hand, all in a trouble-free zone,
   Soon they shall know, and suffer the price,
   Extinct animals, for them shall they mourn.

Parivash Jeelani

POLLUTION

Pollution will be
The death of us all
No escape for any life
No escape at all

We can't say we were not warned
Because that will be untrue
We'll all be responsible
Both me and you

It's so sad
It makes you want to cry
Why are we letting
Our beautiful world die?

Greeny 2000

A Precious Place

This habitat we call a 'rainforest',
is the most precious emerald jewel to me.
Rainforests are not just beautiful places,
they are useful and we should cherish them eternally.

So stop clearing the rainforests haphazardly, and
come; take a look at the treasures
beneath the green tangled tree canopy.

Concealed in the protective arms of the tree branches,
lies, more than a haven for endangered animals.
Open your eyes
and on a closer inspection
you will see,
many rare species of plants are nestled,
protected under the towering guard-like trees.

These plants contain medicines for illnesses,
that can save you and me.
So next time you go to the doctor,
think about where that vital wonder drug originated
that relieves you of your pain!
Bearing that in mind,
when you are about to spray an aerosol,
think about acid rain!

For it's not just the trees that are twisted,
the people who destroy them are too!
The animals close to extinction sit in puzzlement,
they are amazed at what they see us do.
The Raggiana bird of paradise
turns and talks to a lonely tree,
'I know that these humans are supposed to be clever,
but they really don't seem so to me!'

Vicky McHugh

MOOD SWINGS IN NATURE

How starkly gleam the raindrops bright
Jewels that so pretty hang
From tree branches sprawling overhead!
From slanting roof-tops in the night
Hailstones cascading down like missiles
Strike the garden shed.

The hot sun's giant searchlight
Threatens from
The cauldron of the midday sky
Above us. With seething might
The hot earth fetches
A huge seismic sigh.

Where the earth faults, a dragon breathes
Molten fire through
Flared volcanic nostrils
Wide. Out of its great lungs seethes
A sea of noxious lava
That wanton kills.

And from the raging sea enormous waves
Tossed by howling winds
Target lone ships;
Or, rushing overland, poor men's graves
They open up
Amid the battered townships.

Mood swings a blot in nature are.
Not man's swings alone;
In a wider span
More alarming is the new war,
To wit, the threat of global warming
To bionic man.

Angus Richmond

ANYTHING PURE

Purity,
Sweet and innocent,
New spring lambs, waiting to have their throats slit,
The song of the thrush, death to the snail,
The new-born child, tarnished by sin.
Purity drowned,
In a filth-ridden earth.

Purity,
Non-existent,
Soft falling, destructive sulphurous rains,
Acres of countryside, genetically modified,
The infant child, destroyed by knowledge,
Hope extinguished,
And the earth is drowned.

I held the illusion
Something pure existed,
I never found it, is it there to be found?
Has all the earth fallen,
To this mess we now live in
Nobody ever notices,
Anything pure,
Is ridiculed,
Anything pure,
Is it there to be found?

Clare Newsome

YEARS OF HURT

Nothing less for you my world,
I take sleep upon your golden mould,
A thousand moments of heavenly bliss,
As I rocked upon your velvet kiss,
You've always been my shining star,
So what do we do, we *kill* you, with our car.

We transform your life from bad to worse,
The telling tales of years of hurt,
You bear the scars of our crusading wars,
You weep at the thought of all our laws,
Do you remember when we did not live?
At least all that was there did then give.

I have no conscience about your death,
No conscience along with all the rest,
Your clock ticks down with every night,
But I will never believe I'm right.
To bed forever our bleeding stone,
You will never ever be alone.

Robert Dickins (16)

PLEASE LISTEN TO ME

If people would listen to me,
And feel my pain,
Would they let things happen,
That would take my leg,
Or even my life?

What would the people that did this to me
Feel like if their life was rearranged?
Would they plant those bombs,
That can rip off a limb,
Or blow down a house,
In the blink of an eye?

Would all these things happen,
If people would listen to me?

Kayleigh Hardy (14)

GONE BUT NOT FORGOTTEN

In a world where sad people cry
Shedding a tear for Madam Butterfly.
Where lots of homeless people roam
Trying to find the ladybird a home.
A planet of mice and men
Sorrow for poor Jenny Wren.
Sadness everywhere you see
Even Cock Robin can't find a tree.

From Olympus Cupid shot an arrow
To take some love to the dead sparrow.
No more cats or tiny mice
Both are now as cold as ice.
No more leather the tanner to iron
Gone the tiger and the lion.
Empty cages at the zoo
Away the last wasp flew.

No wild dogs left to muzzle
Children never seen a monkey puzzle.
Zebra no rivers left to drink
Shops have all run out of milk.
From powder now we make our wine
In books the only sheep or swine.
Why did we do the animals wrong
Even the poor humble elephant's gone.

Colin Allsop

AN UGLY PLACE

Trees and grass disappear,
The world is turning into an ugly mass of brick and metal,
Surrounded by smoke, noise and pollution.
Where have all the beautiful things gone?
Why?
Because man does not appreciate them,
And we fulfil our greed by destroying the earth.
Soon birds in the early morning sun,
And dolphins in the sea,
Will only be a distant memory.
Nothing at all,
Just people,
Existing alone on an ugly, ugly planet.

Rebecca Butler (17)

Beauty And The Beast

Our earth is truly a wonderful place
But times can be very savage
Provides us with food, shelter and warmth
Then at times will ruin and ravage

Towering mountains covered in snow
Reaching right up to the sky
Mountaineers challenge their dangerous slopes
Alas I'm afraid many die

When she is calm the sea as you know
Can be such a wonderful sight
Sometimes she gets angry, better beware
Her mood can change overnight

Tall graceful trees sway in the breeze
Landscapes which fill you with joy
Sometimes you find nature's unkind
She will often uproot and destroy

Orchards of fruit trees, fields full of corn
To man makes a heart-warming vista
Clouds start to form, then maybe a storm
For we're right in the path of a twister

Fine buildings, theatres, churches and schools
Many things man doth create
But there's always a fear, they'll disappear
When the earth starts to quiver and quake

Picturesque villages, midst olive groves
A smouldering volcano nearby
If ever she blows, everyone knows
Death will rain down from the sky

So temperamental this planet of ours
Has been since life first began
Both beauty and beast she'll never cease
Her constant battle with man.

Peter Webb

SEEING THE UNSEEN

The future of the world is only seen in fantasy.
Yet all I can say is that in reality,
The future to me is what you make of it.
Follow your path and make your own way.
Tomorrow is your clean page.
The book is opened truly at birth
And along the chapters like a diary you fulfil each day
Each step, each minute, every breath you take,
Every thought, every letter I write on this page,
Has been in the future ready to grab
There's a future for everyone, everything, every place,
It is up to you,
You owe it to yourself
To make the best of this sweet hell.

Hannah Cummins (17)

Unfriendly Man

The environment's unfriendly,
But man just makes it worse.
He huffs and puffs to make the rules,
Then goes into reverse.
You try it first, we'll follow,
Says one, and then another.
Initiatives are not for us,
Most promises are hollow.
If all the rest, cleaned off their plot,
'Twould make for a good tomorrow.

J Blades

UN SHORE

Mile upon mile,
sand and tides
rubbing time.
Pebbles smoothed
by the constant move;
as they shift,
rumble,
clank,
and tumble,
gathering sewage and waste,
dropped by those in haste.
The tide will wash away these sins,
but eventually they return,
again.

Amy Phillips

WEEDS

Man, in his pride only sees beauty
in his own creation: in the well
trimmed shrub, and the garden
flowers, standing row on row.

Whence this urge to tame the Earth?
To regulate and regiment? To
replace the fields of meadowsweet
with endless, arid fields of wheat?

It was never God's intention
for man to uproot His creation:
to foul the earth and air and water:
to force the earth to yield yet more.

It is not part of some divine plan
to make wasteful glut, while
millions starve. It is man's
folly and greed.

God's earth is of surpassing beauty,
each creature and plant having its place.
But man must ever tamper, alter:
seeing wilderness as an affront.

When in the blossom of the humble weed:
in the delicate tracery of every leaf,
may be heard the music of the spheres
and be seen the hand of God.

Terry Flower

SEXES ON THE BEACH - GULLS CRY AND BUOYS FLOAT

I knew a boy, kept himself to himself,
Emotions he hid so well,
He let no one in, thought crying a sin,
But his eyes have a story to tell,

If he had one girlfriend, he had two,
Though he thought that love was sappy,
The three words he said, only under his breath in bed,
And only then to keep her happy,

'Emotional retard' his ex's called him,
Behind his back and then to his face,
He bore the brunt and put up a front,
Never cried; the ultimate disgrace,

But I know he turns over memories in his head,
I've seen him blush and cringe,
But he never smiles, while his eyes that beguile,
'Water' at unforgotten things,

I know inside he's tired of the games,
Only punches to prove he can,
Emotion is a girl thing, he neither sinks nor swims,
Keeps afloat with his ego; he's a man.

Lucy Burgan

GIRLS ON BOYS

I adore male company,
I'm not about to lie,
I come across all cute and girlie,
now that I can't deny,
I coax them in,
then spit them out
measly flies in my spider's trap,
oh heavens stop pulling a face there's nothing wrong with that!
It's all about revenge you see,
it's all part of my trick,
and yet these males adore me, how stupid! Ha!
How thick!

I flirt around,
I smile and laugh,
pretending I'm so sweet,
then over my cauldron they feel my wrath,
now not so cute and petite,
I'm sorry for all you boyfriend lovers,
there's nothing I can say,
to think of all their pathetic ways,
amuses me day to day.

Daniela Hardy

THE FIRST DAYS OF BEING SINGLE

Scenes from the night before
Sketch themselves behind my eyes and
Disturb the bottom of my belly.
The politics of being single
Have failed to change in the years I passed with you.
I slipped back into the game as
The cool, slow drink slipped down my throat.
Strobes flashed possibilities into my veins.
Semi-darkness masked my mourning
As I prowled the crowd of hungry specimens,
Brushing and pushing through hot, eager bodies
Made my flesh flush.
My clothes began to burn my skin.
Shivers crept up my skirt and
Covered my chest.
You left, and left your sex with me.

Erin Halliday

SOULMATE

God in his wisdom created
male and female.
Man and woman.
We read in the bible God took a
rib from man to create woman.

God installed in all living things an inborn desire
to attract and be courted by the opposite sex.
Be it fish, bird, cattle, creepy crawlers and beasts great
and small, this natural and normal instinct exists.

It was God's intention for man to have a helper and partner
to share the rough and the smooth, laughter and tears.
God created each individual with a lifespan for living, loving,
learning, and to value the essence of time, so precious and dear.

People the world over are searching for their own true love,
longing for a special partner and soulmate.
Perhaps a handsome man, with a twinkle in his eye, sense of humour,
charm, whatever the attraction, draws them together,
and seals their fate.

The opposite sex adds a touch of spice and sparkle to our busy
often hectic lives.
Without them we would neither be proud caring mothers, or
devoted partners and wives.

What nicer than being wined and dined by our favourite man be it
sweetheart or husband.
Pampering us with affection, we feel special, and in our chiffon and
beaded ensemble feminine and grand.

I am heaven blest to have a loving husband and three handsome
grown-up sons, and how I revel in their male company.
They certainly keep me young at heart and blissfully happy,
I believe, to show love and respect promotes peace and harmony.

Elizabeth Myra Crellin

THE TRUTH ALWAYS COMES THROUGH

Men have got a lot to answer for,
Many of them walk through the door,
When they can not cope and think it's the answer
They run away thinking they are the master.

What a laugh! This is a coward's act
They leave you with children, not turning back.
A shed tear on someone's shoulder
Then get on with their life, not facing the fact.

They avoid responsibility to help you live
Running away as if they have you to forgive.
Living a lie, as if on the run
But for the wife and siblings it is no fun.

There may be two sides to every story
But there's only the truth which has its glory
Because one day another partner will realise
Before taking him on, they should open their eyes.

Sheralee Le-Gros

WATERFALL OF TEARS

Just when I thought my life was complete
Something has to go wrong
I'm not allowed happiness
I knew it wouldn't last long.

People are always doing this
They let me fall deep
Then they decide I'm not good enough
And leave me to weep.

All I want is love in my life
Is that too much to ask?
Just for one person to care for me
It seems like such a task!

I'm destined for a lifetime alone
It's the way it's meant to be
A life full of sadness and hurt
Is what God has planned for me.

Charlotte Cook

THE DREAM TRAIN

The train chugs by in the starlit night,
Soon it will be morning, soon it will be light.
It is called the train that never sleeps,
Though all its passengers are sleeping deep.
It whistles on into the depths of the night,
All essence of reality becomes far out of sight.
The train is the source of all your dreams,
As you clamber aboard the driver's face beams.
He knows that dreams are your escape from reality,
Your escape from the coldness and corruption of humanity.
Next time you draw your curtains on the night sky,
Think of the dream train as it rambles on by.
Dreams are not simply signs of an over-active imagination,
You will come to realise they are your one true salvation.

Elaine Walklet

BLUE

When I shed a tear,
I don't dry it.
When I feel a rage,
I don't deny it.
I don't fear love,
For love is a craving,
I know why I am blue,
I crave the love of you.

Sara Harris

SPURNED LOVER

I'm alone, reflecting over my lover's treachery.
With moistened eyes, vivid images of
perfidious exploits intensify.

Possible phantom slaughter of lover pervades
tortured mind and imagined revenge is soothing
and lazy clock ambles at leisure.

In alcoholic haze, unclear eyes peek
into glowing fire coals which dance
sensually, souvenirs of former passions.

Visions of fresh lover are amplified,
and grow into crescendo of fresh hatred
which pelts the brain like peas.

Befuddled brain, confused, without conviction
seeks a permanent solution to unplanned betrayal.
Crunching minutes pass as potent capsules
are consumed in haste.

A Branthwaite

HE WAS BORN TODAY

It was the evening before the night
When Jesus was born into the light
Heavenly angels walked round and round
Yet none walked o'er the ground
They looked towards heaven that stretched afar
To all blessed souls upon God's great star
They looked through forests hidden where
Wintry leaves hung dead on God's air
Angels looked seawards where they found
It all frozen over and fishes lay bound
Yet in the sky heavenly birds still flew
In feathered harmony they kissed the dew
Angels asked why so silent their call
Then angels whispered to one and all
Then an angel asked where shall we find
The wondrous man who is all of mankind
For he is all both farthest and nearest
The highest, the lowest of all men the dearest
Then the angels found the way to the light
Following God's star towards Jesus that night
The angels came to a stable all forlorn
Where sweet baby Jesus that night was born
He lay in a manger among cattle and sheep
Safe from harm sweet Jesus did sleep
Then birds began to sing their sweet refrain
That the son of God would spread his name
Now everywhere the angels went they cried
He is love, he is life and all who have died

Ann Hathaway

Deepest, Darkest Fathoms

He returns again, this evening,
So strong, so tall, so sure.
I watch through hidden curtains,
As he walks, he sits, he talks.

His hair, so dark, like velvet,
Falls forward and hides,
The deepest, darkest fathoms,
Of a pair of tawny eyes.

Nothing of me, he knows,
No name, no face, no path.
I watch him and I covert him,
In secret and bitter sight.

He towers over others,
My knight of deepest night.
His craggy face, his silken voice,
Are all I see with light.

Patricia Cunningham

A Walk In The Woods

The narrow lane winds its way between whispering trees,
Shafts of sunlight etching the rustling leaves with a touch of gold,
The sturdy oaks stand straight and tall,
While aspen trees shimmer with delight,
Blackbird and thrush sing their deep-throated love songs
Lovingly to each other,
A colourful woodpecker hammers away diligently
Preparing a home for his family,
Rabbits and hares play hide and seek in the nearby meadow
While in the distance, a young deer, grazes in peaceful solitude.
Wild roses and honeysuckle bedeck the hedgerows
Yellow headed primroses, cowslips and buttercups
Peep between the long green grasses,
On a tall tree top, a lone nightingale serenades the sunset
With her lilting love song,
The glittering fragment of a rainbow, promises a new day,
The woodland sleeps, peacefully.

Wendy Dawson

DREAM ON

Strawberry ribbons tease the sensual mind
Flickering about her sun-drenched golden sheen
Heart bursting emerald eyes
Reflecting life's shimmering crystal stream
Sylph-like adorning cornflower blue
Swirling emotions into romantic dreams
Creation's garment suddenly fully sequinned
Pray leave me here a while to gaze
Her form to stay with me all my days.

Roger S Foster

HYPOTHESISING

'If you could have your life again, and make a change at all',
Is a burning question in my mind, looking back when I was small.
Why was I born in thirty-nine and not in eighty-four?
I wouldn't be very old and maybe not so poor.

Why was I born in Hampshire and not the south of Spain?
I might have been a pirate and sailed the Spanish main.
I could have danced Flamenco, or faced a raging bull,
Instead I work for a pump firm, and drive to work from Poole.

I could have had rich parents, been born with a silver spoon.
I might have been a Lord now, or perhaps been to the moon.
But we lived in a railway house, the windows always rattled,
When the Mail train went through early, and neighbours tittle tattled.

Why was I born so healthy, and christened another Brian?
Why did I go to Grammar school, and have to keep on trying?
If I had lived in America, I would not have met my wife,
I would have driven a Chrysler, had a very different life.

I would not have my children, or friends that I hold dear,
I might not have spoken English, or had a pint of beer.
I could have been a gypsy, or an orphan or a mute,
It's fun to hypothesise, but I was dealt this suit.

B M Hurll

SCHOOL DAYS

Come on, move it, you'll be late
Your pals are waiting by the gate
Where's that scarf I said to wear?
Are you sure you've combed your hair?

Now come straight home after school
Please hurry up, don't act the fool
I know, I know, you're nearly ten
Please, please don't start that again!

I know you're going to tell me how
You're old enough and grown-up now
Come on, come on, or you'll be late
Do you know it's nearly half past eight!

Yes, yes, I know about tonight
But ask your dad if it's alright
If he says yes then you can go
With your friends to that picture show.

Right off you go - don't bang the door
Don't I get kisses anymore?
Take care sweetheart, here's your bus fare
Be good sunshine, take care, take care.

G G Swepstone

A Hero's Farewell

Don't cry my dear heart, it is time I depart,
Let me go in joy and in grace,
I've fulfilled my part, to leave is an art,
So wipe those tears off your face.

I have carried my share with trials to spare,
Bravely plodding along all the way,
My cross I did bear with love and with care
And let barking dogs have their say.

Now my course is all set, I don't really regret
Things left undone or unsaid,
I'm not broken yet and am willing to bet
That a life that's well lived isn't dead.

So let me move on, and after I'm gone
Remember with gladness and glee
The light in your life that actively shone
And the wonder of you and of me.

And know that we'll meet and once again greet
In a land that's more glorious than this,
I'll reserve you a seat, reunions are sweet
In the gardens where spirits know bliss.

Emmanuel Petrakis

CLINGING ELIAN

Clinging
To his mother tightly, clasping her around the neck,
Elian Gonzales and mummy sat upon the deck,
Sailing from their country, Cuba, in an overcrowded boat,
Heading to America with democratic vote.

The rowboat began to sink, submerge into the sea,
Suddenly capsizing, they were jettisoned debris.
His mother recognised her weakening, this was her life countdown,
She looped tyre inner tube over her son's head, poor swimmer,
                                             bound to drown.
Her final struggle with this action took all her energy,
'Take care of him!' she gasped
'Get him to my family!'
These requests expended her few and final breaths,
She slipped under the waves, plunging down into the depths.
An eddy surged, then broken ocean smoothed
And flattened evenly, as life and swell were soothed.

Clinging,
Her traumatised son clasped the tube with all his might,
Clinging,
For two tormented days and everlasting nights,
Thankfully on Thanksgiving Day scooped up by devout fisherman
Photographed clinging to him, front page news, Elian.

Two divisions erupted, conflict within his clan,
Kin wanted him in America, his father, home in Cuba with him,
                                                      a Cuban.
Spattering exploded into a raging fire, government involved
                                                with the FBI
To restore son to father, used tear gas, gunman pointed a gun
                                                from his thigh
At Elian who was cowering, clinging again to devout fisherman,
And screaming, 'Help me!' in pre-dawn raid which caused
                                     public reprimand.

'It was to curb family trouble!' explained FBI. A deed so inglorious!
                                                                               Why oh why?
Shabby treatment to a boy who had suffered so much and
                              watched his mother founder and die.

Hilary Jill Robson

THE NEW POSTMAN

Have you ever thought of the postman's lot,
When new at the game, and not so hot?
In towns we find, the houses in rows,
But here in the village, well . . . goodness knows!
   Down the lane and round the back,
     Where's the front door? And no letter box Jack!
Council houses, what a lark!
Hunt for the number, it's in the dark!
At the top of the door, under porch roof -
Why not on the gate, you silly goof?
Postman mutters, as he wends his way,
   String on the gate, to keep children at bay!
   Dogs at the ready, mind your leg, Jack!
   Give him a toffee, and don't turn your back!
   Slots in the door, with springs so new
   Letters jump back, and the air is 'blue' -
Sometimes he thinks, while the job has its charms
It would be much easier, if he had three arms!
It's life in the raw, and all that fresh air
Keeps a person in trim, with friends everywhere!

Katherine Fell

ONLY A NAME?

Is a name very important?
A title we are given at birth.
I think if we were a number,
I wonder what we'd be worth!

Well I've given teddy a name,
For he is my special friend.
He does keep all my secrets,
Yes, I know it's just pretend!

But animals have names too,
And answer to their call.
We call them ridiculous things,
I wonder if they feel a fool!

Objects have a name like a mug,
Why everything really has a title.
So is my name really special then or,
Just lumbered when I was very small?

I wonder what one could use then,
As we all are really special I know.
I guess, one way to look at it,
At least our name gets bigger as we grow!

Ann Beard

PERHAPS I'LL WRITE A POEM

I think I'll write a poem what shall it be?
Perhaps some prose, I suppose but who knows?
Should it rhyme in time mine would be a crime.
Perhaps I'll write a sonnet, if you want it.
But if you prefer, I'll ban it or bin it.
I tried a quatrain, with much pain, 'twas in vain.
Do you need a high IQ for a haiku?
I'll try a few and forget - the couplet.
What about an elegy, maybe you'll see.
My blank verse is a dank curse, even rank worse.
I'll seize the similes, pause for metaphors.
I'll get to the root of an iambic foot.
My ballad will be sad, my epic is quick.
I'll write a stanza - about Mario Lanza.
I'm so sorry about my allegory.
Sweeter than music, maybe is my lyric.
I could cram with epigrams and load with odes.
I forgot a bon mot, I'll forego a bon mot.
Perhaps I will write a poem, no perhaps not.

Terry Daley

TIME TO SHOO!

Morning sky - dippity doo!
Clouds going by - in the blue;
In my eye - nothing new;
Soon I'll die - so will you;

'I'm a flicker - I'm a flame;
No high kicker - just a name;
Keep the wicker - that's the aim;
Banter bicker - whence you came'

Morning sky - dippity doo!
Clouds gone by - in the blue;
Blink your eye - miss your cue;
One big lie - time to shoo!

Tom Ritchie

SECOND WORLD WAR -
3RD SEPTEMBER '39 TO 8TH MAY '45

Memory Lane is still leading me back
To those desperate years when the days were so black;
When sirens were sounding and people were scared -
To their shelters they fled when war was declared.

British cities were bombed, buildings fell to the ground.
Destruction was rife, stones and bricks all around.
Theatres and churches gone, little was spared
In those terrible raids after war was declared.

I stood with my father on a hill top at night
And saw for myself such a heart-rending sight;
Widespread devastation, the fire and the flame
Which destroyed our city and brought it to shame.

Brave men on the home front gave of their all
To bring food, drink and shelter, and answer each call.
Seeing families made homeless with dearest ones dead
Was a sorrowful sight with streams of tears shed.

There seemed no ending - the war still raged free,
More killings at home and ships lost at sea.
Soldiers, sailors and airmen lost their lives in the fight;
Oh God - never again must we face such a plight.

After five years of warfare, victory came fast.
The scourge of battle was over at last!
Americans and Poles were going quite mad -
Throwing bottles and shouting; the scene was quite sad.

But when VE night passed, and daylight broke through
A new life began, and peace dawned anew.
We will never forget the millions who died,
They gave their lives for this country and 'turned the tide'.

From conflict to peace - that is how it must stay;
Let's recapture the glory of that eighth day in May.

Joyce Hemsley

OUR WORLD TODAY

Our world today is in a terrible state,
Can't something be done before it's too late?
Before all is destroyed by hatred and greed,
Working with nations for this to succeed.

If all the money spent on war and strife,
Could be channelled into making for a better life,
How different the victims' lives would be,
Living happily and from want and trauma free.

Surely it's not too much for us to ask,
That all Christian people should join in the task,
Of helping to make this world a better place,
And this can be done with God's good grace.

So take up the challenge, work with this end in view,
Ask the Lord to show us what we can do.
To make men realise the need for peace,
And a change of heart for conflict to cease.

E K Jones

My Greatest Loss
(A tribute to my late wife)

I walk through the valley of shadows
After a lifetime of happiness
My dear one has now departed
And I'm left with emptiness

Through joy, sometimes tears, we travelled
Always there, by each other's side
Living for one another
Whatever life should betide

The happiness I get from our children
Whose mother they've lost too
Sustains me in my greatest loss
For without them I'd not get through

So if you are in this position
Remember as you grieve and despair
There are others whose lives are similar
And who think of you and care

And if you have lost a loved one
And your thoughts are racked with pain
Remember it's not forever
But till you meet again

Martin Selwood

A Walk On The Wild Side

How does it start?
It starts with a sunny day, blue skies and a slight chill in the air
Warm clothing like a fleece,
Walking boots and energy
The imagining starts you off and then;
To walk along the cliff top beside the golf course
Up and down the uneven grassy banks
Chatting as you go.
Looking at the sea down below
It's exciting and exhilarating.
Wide skies, windy gusts wrapping you round
And a blue Norfolk sea!
So much more beautiful than grey!
One is transported to personal memories as you go.
Walking back along the seashore, stepping over stones
Watching the crab boats
You would like the walk to go on forever
But it can't, legs tire and time passes on
Pleasure and joy start here
Unrivalled.

Hazel Cooper

The ABC Of My Love For Chocolate

Chocolates, milk and plain, dark and white;
Aromatic air, attracting an allegro accord
Beautiful bonbon, bronzed and burnished
Created with cream, coated and clothed;
Designed by desire, a dream of destiny;
Euphonic ecstasy, expression of elixir
Fortissimo fudge, fondant fantasia;
Growing gusto, greeting gratification
Heavenly harmonic, handsome and handmade;
Inhaled incense, intense interpretation
Jazzy jaunty jelly, joyous jamboree;
Kissable kernel, kind of kaleidoscope
Lovely and lucious, laid in luxury
Melody of milk, moments of madness;
Naked nuts nestling, noisette nirvana
Operatic occasion, orchestrate options
Pungent and perfumed, psalm of paradise;
Quiet quaver, quality of quaintness
Rich and redolent, rhapsody of rapture;
Sure and satisfying, scented sweetness
Truffle of temptation, tastebuds tickled;
Undisputed union, Utopia unwrapped
Voluptuous vocal variations, velvet virtuoso;
Worth waiting for this winsome wonder
XYZ, the alpha and omega is chocolate.

Jean Wearn Wallace

A Say On Words

Perfection pickles the heart and mind,
To the n'th degree so as not to find,
Any resource left in time of need,
So tight in fact or future lead.

Not a granule is left at stake,
To anew a cause or to make
Something concrete, even a part
As indefinite as a dart.

Into the realm of make-believing,
For to seize your chance and relieving,
In hope there is an opening somewhere
Maybe any place here or there.

But when all doors of opportunity are lost
By closure at relative low cost,
Figure out what the accumulation has meant,
If all ways and means have been gone and sent.

In matching style of closure and crystal,
For the sands of time will crack like pistol,
No longer presently be on tap,
To do something else from distance as on map.

For the die is cast,
At nature's full blast,
There is no second chance,
Heed this for truth is as straight as a lance.

N Lemel

THE KISS

Everyone in life,
who was troubled by strife,
you can bet that they were betrayed
with a kiss.

Since the master of the world
had his wish for us unfurled,
he has forged this little hitch,
did he mean it to turn into such a glitch?

That before our bed is made,
and we come out from the shade,
you can bet that we'll be betrayed
with a kiss.

We would all just rather fight,
feel our enemies wrath and might,
but you can bet he will betray us
with a kiss.

Maybe this world was made,
to be just a masquerade,
where everyone betrays you
with a kiss.

Or, have we just been cursed,
with a spell that's well rehearsed,
for our imminent betrayal
with a kiss.

As we take what life can throw,
bear up well under the blow,
out there someone's waiting for us
with that kiss.

Jean Paisley

NONE BUT YOU

Pierce the shell
Burst the yolk
The thing won't mind
It can't even move
Never mind struggle
If you look closely
You can see its . . .
Its eyes are open
Its hands are pleading
Almost praying
The air bubbling rising to the occasion
The whole family are gathered round
Faces seem to be one visage.
Strange how our heart rates hasten,
How the flannel is always red-moist
And unclean.
Veins tie these petite frailties taught.

Lee Grace

UNFORGOTTEN SACRIFICE

We, of tender age in this day
feel the burden of freedom.
We search for foe to confront with, raising a
flag and a voice of passion.
We know little of real opposition, we can not
ever know of this.
Our views of black and white stills and fraying
books of history, satisfy our duty to remember.
Please lest we forget the real pain, the lifeless
wreckage of our own clan, the sacrifice.
How do we remember you?
How do we reward your gift to us all?
I heard something that humbled me the other day . . .
You sold your medal, it paid a bill.

I reflect on this profoundly and I realise your worth.

Michael Smith

A Heart Of Gold, A Life Of Sin

Ashamed, estranged,
Becoming deranged,
Feels like maybe you,
Need a change,
From this overwhelming,
Sunshine, unto the pouring rain.

A summer's day, with a winter's wind.
A heart of gold,
A life of sin,
When nearing the end, you may win,
But in reality you wish it didn't begin.
More laughs, maybe more fun,
Someone might have told you,
When it begun.

Think of what you've not yet done
Before you pull the trigger of that gun,
To disappear before your time,
Is so unfair and hard to define.

Hang in there, give it all you've got,
This chance may be your only shot,
Enjoy a little, enjoy the lot,
Free your mind, don't let it rot,
Don't be the one that time forgot!

Donna Marie Hardie

OUR PLIGHT

Disease filters and soaks the streets
Blood stenches vile the summer heat
Nature grinds helplessly bitter sweet song
Hours while away our hopeless agony
Long gone are the veil of tears that once weighed down our eyes
No longer we contemplate wrong nor right
For the powder and metal of bullets and bombs have fulfilled their duty
Blasting apart the voice of critic, activist and confused
So darling daughter of mine what else of our plight
Now that oxygen pollutes your bloodstream in this your life
How long before you too dance along to the tune of bloodshed
                                                      and violence

Tell me
How long

Saheeda Khan

A Has-Been Madam

Pink clashing with orange,
dressed like a light show.
I see you're wearing that fur again,
people get shot for less in America!
Your roots are showing.
Those ear-rings dangle a shade
too much like chandeliers.
By the way, don't you realise paste is passé?
Has anyone ever told you that shade
of lipstick doesn't suit you!
Certain men are drawn to you
like lemmings to a clifftop.
Do they think you're still on the game?
They are prey - mere flies lured to your web centre,
but you are the victim.
People laugh, but they are mocking,
noting with disdain the stale
smell of cheap gin on your breath.
Funny how your mouth never closes yet
nothing comes out only smutty innuendo.
Do you ever read the papers?
Why can't you say something intelligent?
You fail to see the cracks emerge
in your tarnished veneer.
Perhaps the mirror image is blurred
by too much mascara.
Tell me, what is it you fear?

John Taylor

Final Darkness

Difference of opinion, of faith and of creed.
Affects all of us but mainly the ones most at need.
As the movement rolls on for the right to speak,
The promises of leaders mean less to the weak.

We're forced to watch images of flat, barren land.
Fallen cities lay before us, built on bloodied sand.
As the men give their orders to go for your guns,
The boys say goodbye to their cherished loved ones.

Standing in rows upon the front line.
There in body - but not in mind.
Trained to believe to do as they're told,
All they want to do is grow old.

Hungry bellies - rivers of tears.
Our boys battle on, hiding their fears.
Remembering the briefings and all of the lies,
Visions of hope fade through smoke-filled sad eyes.

If strong we could stand up and shout out 'No more.'
'Just leave us something that's worth fighting for.'
But as a world we are weak and we fall to our knees,
Begging to someone to stop this please.

The day soon gives up, followed my night.
No darkness surrounds us, only one great bright light.
After an eternity the gunfire has finally ceased -
We now watch the sun as it sets in the east.

Helen Riley

CHANT

A star is a hole in the night.
The cities hide the stars.
The cities hide the night.
The cities hide the day.
The day hides the stars.
The day is the city.
The city is the day.
There are no holes in the day.
Only the night promises freedom.

Athol Cowen

The Marriage

Evening clouds willingly bare their souls,
a thin veil to be searched, revealing
hungry stars ready to be set free, to
invade the sky, hanging by untied threads,
bobbing over momentary harmony below.

Side by side, the earth and its sometime
adversary, the surrounding sea, lie dormant,
together, peacefully asleep, entwined in a
soft embrace; constant companions, whether
times be fraught or calm.

A slight sigh raises soothing undulations;
fragrant perfumes, that reach out and touch
each other, affectionately. Like lovers making up
after yesterday's quarrel, each delicate
caress made with warmth and tenderness.

Daylight opens the closed curtains of
the night before, turning over the next
page of the book, unveiling a gathering,
a marriage, of the elements, consummated
by fire and passion as a distant storm brews.

G Clarke

RED ROSE (OF LIFE)

She caught my eyes one morning
Ever since I've sat there watching
In her own grace of time she grew
Gently opening her heart
It was such a wonder to watch her as she bloomed . . .

Then one morning when I peeped at her
she stood there more beautiful than ever
that she snatched this heart of mine
She smiled at me, I smiled back to her
Her perfume danced into my nose
as a possessed lover I stared into her . . .

Days went by
Slowly she began to fade
taking every bit of my heart with her
She smiled no more
There was only tears in my eyes as I watched her go . . .

Truly I missed her
Her beauty, her smile, her sweet perfume . . .

She left me stranded here
As I could grieve no more
I turned my head around
a small glow pieced into my eyes
from behind the bushes

A young soul blushing in red
Nope, I've not noticed her before
for I've been so in love with one
Sweet, gentle and red
She is
as my dear one once before . . .

Why . . . shouldn't I be in love again?

Jiwamalar Perumal

RETRIBUTION

You lit the fire
Then left me with the flame;
What must I do,
To put it out again?

You took the lock,
Left me with broken key:
What must I do,
Now all is closed to me?

You broke the links,
Which held life's golden chain:
Where should I go,
To find such links again?

The wounds of love,
Leave marks which lie untold:
God alone knows,
The salve for sicken'd souls.

Knolly La Fortune

PICTURE ON THE WALL

A picture hangs
In the room on the wall
The old gentleman
Remembers once upon a time before.

The pretty lady
With the hour-glass figure
Sadly today needs a zimmer frame.

Memory Lane
Walking down Memory Lane
You can walk down the lane
For hours at a time
Remembering yesterday
As if yesterday is today.

T Lawrence

SPACE LIES

I was listening to the radio
   about America probing space
and what I heard was amazing
   and a diabolical disgrace

The recent satellite that went missing
   was anything but right
it had a fault of which they knew
   yet still launched it into flight

They claimed they didn't wish the public
   to know that they had failed
but surely this is insanity
   with the money that's entailed

They also said that modern youth
   with space travel all are keen
so they didn't want to let them down
   to show faults in their machine

Lachlan Taylor

THE POST

Waiting under cover of darkness:
concentrated contemplation,
anticipating interruption
of the dormant home.
The thud of promise
on the dog-eared doormat
cuts the tension.
Time then to emerge
from my downy hideaway;
pluck up courage,
saunter surreptitiously towards the door,
casting a casual glance
towards the envelopes of pledge
or disappointment
scattered litter-like across the floor.
Eyes scanning deftly
the static buff and white portends;
bills and statements,
declarations of disaster and love;
determined to locate
those happy letters signifying
Me.
Alighting with triumph and delight
upon an outline deliciously familiar and sublime,
deliberately delivered.
Hungry I settle on the ageing seat
- having deftly flicked the kettle, lit the grill -
for I only ever contemplate my morning post
in the company of real coffee
and a slice of granary toast.

Julia Murphy

Shadow Man

Fickle finger of fortune
In the kitchen at home
A shadow man watches
Time was left was private

World of peace or education
More teaching of foreigners
A shadow man comments on all
What was that feeling of fear

A gut reaction, a need to please
Those who care on top of us
A shadow man waves a gun
Joy in my heart, peace drops slowly

S M Thompson

LIVE A HOLY LIFE

this existence is hard
so more harder now
why is life not
so very easy now
it's all the same
exactly as it was
before all this
came into being
and was there
the rigidity of existence
is ourselves knowing that
one single purpose that
so lies ahead
ahead of us all
again we walk that
same path like before
where can we go
we must have hope
to do just good
dark empty badness is
deep deep deep vileness
under God's wise laws
we must live lives
so very near perfect
there must be dignity
and much understanding
that's the way forth
to truth and understanding

Richard Clewlow

WHOSE HOUSE?

Mrs Edrich is passing round the collection plate.
She's such a gossip, she's sure to be late.
Mrs Foster's so worried about the flowers,
She's been rearranging them for hours.
And would you believe that Mr Brown can't
find where he's laid the hymn sheets down.
'Oh we'll have to use the old ones,' he cries,
'Someone's bound to criticise.'
Mrs Hammond says she must have the best
cups for coffee and tea.
She likes to have everything just right you see.
I do hope Mr Chapman won't wear his bright green
jacket today.
It's not right in church, to dress that way.
Now I must answer that knock upon the church door.
I wish they'd stick to service times and not arrive before.
I open up and there stands God, as I can plainly see.
Who in his bright green jacket says
'Hello, remember me?'
I can see you're all so busy doing all your chores.
I seem to spend millenniums knocking on people's doors.
I promise if you let me in, to be as quiet as a church mouse.
I think you'll find that this place, used to be my *house*.

Susan Sutherland

How *Stoopid* Can Men Get?

'Avin' bin up a' night wi' toddler'n 'is teeth
I can tell yer it wur a reet relief
When 'ubby said e'd take 'im ta duck pond
Ee aye, our little lad's reet fond

It gi' me a chance ta make dinner ready
An' ta let mi time go well, reet steady
Then 'ome 'ubby came sat down wi' paper
An' it wasn't until later

Wi' both felt that someat were wrong somehow
But wi just 'adn't realized till now
Asked 'im 'try' - as he picked up his cap, and
Try remember wot 'ad 'appened

'Let's see now' he started, 'we stood feedin' ducks
An I could swear, that's a' that 'appened chucks'
Couldn't believe 'e'd walked 'ome wi' empty pram
An' never even missed our Sam

'Well, I don' know like, I know once, 'e were there'
Said 'ubby - then 'See, a' I did love were
Look at mi' watch an' thowt I'd better dash
E'en I thowt there'd bin - a big splash!'

Barbara Sherlow

A Toast To British Pubs

Our pubs are hubs of the grinding wheels
Of busy British life.
Our pubs are where we go knee-searching
For our depleted, spent-up spirits.
Our pubs are the hives where housewives
And husbands do talk freely, as tacit equals.

We drink, and blink, and think,
Sit and soak up potent pep and, when bubbling fit,
Spit out all brands of suppressed shit,
Oft back from near abandonment's brink.
We discuss and debate and decide
On fronds and facets of national pride;
Formulate *sober* and sensible goals to guide
Our state on public issues - some deep, some wide.
We plot our plays, compose our songs;
Sell our products, seal our deals;
Form bands, shake hands;
Siphon out secret facts; iron out contracts;
Patch up, with pacts; and, thus we pleasingly interact
In . . . our . . . own . . . pubs.

Where else can we live our lives but in pubs?
Not in our homes. Oh no. Not there!
Our homes are just there for recrimination,
Reproduction, resignation, and incubation.

So, come on girls and boys. Let's toast
This, greatest of all British institutions -
Our good old local, the pub!

Kopan Mahadeva

I Held Spring In My Hand

I held spring in my hand, I felt it in the breeze, touched it
while lying outstretched in the sun but fragile as it was,
like a snowdrop kneeling on the earth to kiss the land,
I could have let it go, let it slip through the fingers of my lazy hands
and then, like the moon's dove, knew that as quick as it had come
and fluttered on me feathered softness, feathered love,
it would go with the stinging heat of the bee in the rose to comfort me.

Emma-Louise Cartwright

DEGENERATION GAP

My employer got her sums wrong -
found she could not 'compete',
yet it is I who waves 'So long!'
To drag away redundant feet.

Luxury car still in her 'drive' -
half-mile long, lined with yew;
huge country house is yet her own -
no bloody, leeching mortgage due.

Gardener trims extensive grounds,
as we clip our budget -
repairing clothes, counting bread-rounds;
JSA? How they begrudge it!

I had no choice - I had to go
(thirty years of service!)
victimised for what? - I don't know;
No wonder workers are nervous!

Now there she goes, the selfish jerk -
graft low, and income high -
whilst I, though deemed too old for work,
oddly - it seems - too young to die!

Phoenix Martin

INSOMNIA

Night after night the insomnia comes callin'
my thoughts take me to the land of dread
I close my eyes, I feel myself fallin'
as I toss and turn alone in my bed
I pull the sheets so close up tight
as I try to think a happy thought
I wish the insomnia to vanish clear out of sight
as to this is what the nightmare has brought.

Stacey Quimby

COHEN'S SONG

Since you're gone
The sun's forgotten
How to shine
Feels like it's raining
All the time
And moonlight
Ain't a friend of mine
Since you're gone
Since you're gone
The house is wrecked
And the wine is strong
I drink too much
And I sleep too long
And the birds keep singing
Cohen's song
Cohen's song
Cohen's song
Every day
The same damn song
Cohen's song
Cohen's song
The birds keep singing
Cohen's song

Rod Trott

THE AUTUMN TANKARD
(Dedicated to memories of Brendan Makenna)

When autumn blows in my memory turns round
To a sweet distant time with brown leaves on the ground
I look at my tankard up there on its shelf
To the fondest memories with Brendan I delve

I was sitting at home when dear Brendan came in
Bearing a tankard with widest of grins
He brewed autumn ale with cider and egg
And sweet autumn spices topped off with nutmeg

We drank the good ale, in our head the spice ran
Suffused with its charms the magic began
We gazed out the window and there we did see
Squirrels and elves bounding down a great tree

The autumn leaves spun into corn flakes of gold
Russet brown, red, yellow orange then rolled
Transformed into sprites dancing high in the air
With fairy boys chasing them free from all care

Inspired by the sights that had sprung from the ground
We both began singing and weaving around
An apple tree wassailing carolling rune
To thank mystic autumn for singing its tune.

Brendan's departed his spirit has gone
That mad mystic day in my memory lives on
The tankard stands up there, in autumn I fill
With good autumn ale to his memory drink still

Roy Millar

Rainbows

There is a dark secluded place where in
The winter of their discontent they just
Flee the world. They look to their laurel leaves
And hug, warmed by the fires of coal and lust.

They toast their love with tea and buttered scones,
Whilst outside the trees sough to rough trade winds.
Refugees from those that cast cruel stones
At lovers unrepentant for their sins.

They are convicts of their conviction. They hope
That when they die they occupy whatever space
Is granted, allocated, to those who tried to cope;
Deceiving, grieving, dreaming: rainbows in grace.

Peter Huggins

CLONED

Here comes
My other half,
So like me
It's quite a laugh.
When I see him
On the street,
It's as if I'm going
Me to meet.
The girls are puzzled
Too, you see;
Is it Tweedledum
Or Tweedledee?
And when we gaze
Into their eyes,
Some small confusion
Does arise.
Hip, hip, hip,
But not hooray -
The likeness can
Get in the way.
But it never bothers us,
And life is oh, such fun,
When people really can't decide -
Which one is the one!

V B D'Wit

ONWARD TO 2000

Here we stand upon the threshold of 2000,
But at mid-century where did we stand?
Half the world stood in mortal fear,
Some indeed who were impaled
Upon the thorns of desolation.
Likening one might say to the crown
Of thorns that lay on the head
of our Blessed Saviour.
There strode upon this Earth,
A force unparalleled in evil.
The mark of Satan surely there revealed.
Come let us promise to live our lives
In tolerance, love and peace,
So that we, at last, go forward
To a brave new world, for which
Our forefathers laid down
Their very *lives*.

Andrew Sutherland

SEA OF DAFFODILS

Within the turquoise sea's glassy swell
Daffodils drift.
Silken petals wave, waver
Like fragile wings of butterflies
Drowning.

Rocked by tender combs,
Unblown by barbarous winds
They sleep away, are borne away,
A golden shoal, transformed to leafy green
In the zircon deeps.

Shadows flee before flowering clouds,
Bleed violets across the gentling waves.

With ebbing tide and ebbing day
Blue-glass sky inherits blue-glass sea.
Cloud ripples part, swim into bunches
Of aerial fish, tinted by the fallen sun
To daffodil yellow.

      Or the sky

           Is a sea

                Of daffodils.

Joan Strong

THE TUNNEL OF LOVE

There is light at the end of the tunnel,
There's a life after this one you know,
There is light at the end of the tunnel,
And someday that's where you will go.

You will be floating over your body,
Then into the darkness you'll go,
But be not afraid,
Soon the darkness will fade,
And then you will see the glow.

The light that you see is the light of love,
'Tis the spirit world that you see,
It's that special place that God keeps,
Where at last you will be free.

There's a light at the end of the tunnel,
There's a life after this one you know,
First your body will die,
And then like a sigh,
Into the light you will go.

Ken Gilbert

THE GOLDEN YEARS

Your mum will be one hundred
She has reached her goal at last
Your mum can look forward to the future
And leave behind the past

The Queen Mum will look forward to seeing her daughter every day
And she loves her daughter Elizabeth
In a special sort of way

Queen Elizabeth will look forward to the year 2002
On that day she'll invite her mum round for tea
To celebrate her Golden Jubilee

Queen Elizabeth has reigned over us for fifty years
Most were happy but a few with tears
Queen Elizabeth you are so sweet and kind
You will always be in our thoughts and always in our minds

Queen Elizabeth has done her best for all of you
There's one more duty our loving Queen will do
Is to be with her mum who is one hundred and two

I hope in my heart this all comes true
On that special day I'll hang out the red white and blue
To bless you and show my love for you

Bert Booley

MALTESE MAGIC

Early one morning
Yawning . . .
Awaiting clapped-out bus
Here it comes!
Chug, chug, down the hill
With the maximum of fuss.

On board we clamber
Six at a time
Lights turn to amber
As we begin our climb.

Rattle, clank, thump and splutter
Above the racket we hear our courier utter
'History and Elegance' in Valletta, folks
Sky's dull, the sun'll be hard to coax
Never mind, by the end of the day
Perhaps we'll see a shaft over St Elmo's Bay!

During the week, excitement mounts
The *'Up and Under'* is the trip that counts
Before lunch - activity is above the water line
Afterwards in St Paul's Bay - *'Subterranean is* really fine.

Lobster salad in Bugibba is the best, we're told
Then a climb up Dingli cliffs, if you're really bold
It's said, a day in Gozo's worth two in Crete
There's so much to see - by bus or on feet.

There's fun to be had in Balluta Bay
Eating oyster and crab - cooked the Maltese way
Round off the stay with a night in Naxxar
Next morning - *farewell* - back to Luqa Airport, in the hotel car.

Paul Harvey Jackson

SPRINGTIME

The scene that I now gaze upon,
Simply takes my breath away.
For the cherry tree's in full bloom,
Though the sky is dull and gray.

It's delicate pink blossom,
Is fragrantly so sweet.
Blown by the warmest breeze,
To fall around my feet.

Lasting but a short time,
But giving so much pleasure.
And its splendour will remain,
In my memory to treasure.

Spring is nearly over,
The summer is drawing nigh.
A promise of warmer days,
And cloudless clear blue skies.

But the crisp fresh days of springtime,
Remain eternally in my mind,
And I thank our Heavenly Father,
That He did not make me blind.

M Muirhead

NO IDENTITY

Where are you going to, who are you?
Just a nobody in a zoo
People are strange, adapt to games
So close but yet so far
The hoax that leaves a scar
Yes folks, do you know who you are?
Animal, vegetable, mineral
They're all the bloody same, each one to their own
The cry, the love, the pain
It's all a bloody game what's your name?
When love is a drug ambition is a bug
Dispensable pawn now you are born
Do you like what you see?
In you're no identity.

Joyce

THE CEREMONY

The maiden waited in the tent
Her passion gently stirred.
The ceremony's op'ning drum
Within her heart was heard.

Softly, softly beat the drum, jet black was her hair.
Softly, softly beat the drum, her mind it was not there.

Then in the entrance to the tent
Appeared a figure grand.
With solemn gaze towards the fires
He motioned with his hand.

Slowly, slowly beat the drums, her heartbeat kept apace.
Slowly, slowly beat the drums, such beauty in her face.

Within the circle she did stand
The fires were all around.
The bindings on her hands held fast,
The watchers beat the ground.

Quickly, quickly beat the drums, her eyes gazed far away.
Quickly, quickly beat the drums, this was her special day.

Slow was the sacred knife unsheathed,
In moonlight it did glow,
Was proffered up unto the sky,
'Great spirit, luck bestow.'

Rapid, rapid beat the drums, her body burned as fire.
Rapid, rapid beat the drums, she trembled with desire.

Arced through the air the blade then swung
The watchers gasped with glee.
A stifled cry within her breast -
The bindings then cut free.

Frenzied, frenzied beat the drums, then up a warrior pranced.
Frenzied, frenzied beat the drums, she with her lover danced . .

J G Ryder

KNOWLEDGE V WISDOM

Technology, advancing by the hour,
Unlocks the secrets of the universe
And harnesses its latent, hidden power
To button's touch - a blessing and a curse.

For knowledge, rightly handled, may be used
To bring unbridled blessing to mankind,
But that same knowledge is, alas, abused
By one who harbours evil in his mind.

The problem is, though knowledge can be earned
By reading books and noting what they say,
The wisdom to apply it must be learned
Through life's vicissitudes - no other way!

Without respect for God, all knowledge dies,
For this is where the source of wisdom lies.

Robert A Hardwidge

REFLECTIONS ON PERFECTION

It's late at night
I sit and think of things I could have done
On summer days, before they're gone
Bask in the blazing sun.

But I have found a certain peace
Regardless of the weather
The comfort overwhelms me
Like soft and downy feather.

To find the words that may describe
This wondrous joy of life
Just seems a task impossible
'Complete and utter strife'

But strive I will that you may know
The pleasure I attain
Among the cosy taverns, warm lit,
Sheltered from the rain.

It's poetry and love within
That fills me full of cheer
My love, my deep affection
For a perfect pint of beer.

Les D Pearce

My Grandma's Last Goodbye

There she sat gazing into a flickering glow
That made designs against black chimney brace
Her only TV screen
Crackling of logs her only sonnet
Looking up amazed, she said
'I was thinking about you, my child'
As a withered hand grasped mine
'How are you keeping Grandma?' I asked
'Well I've ploughed a long straight furrow
Trampled on many a stone
I'm finishing off with my windings
I'm on my journey home
Take that ruby jug from the dresser
Go before foul weather sets in
Theirs a blue glow in the fire
Sign of a storm, if I don't see you again my child
We'll meet in Heaven above
Trust in God and keep your powder dry'
With a loving embrace
A lonesome sign, that was to be my gran's
My grandma's last goodbye.

Frances Gibson

PEARLY DAWN

Gentle morning, pearly light,
Moon still loath to hasten flight,
Silence holds the earth in thrall
A blackbird sweetly sings his call;
The watcher's heart beats low,
In time with life's soft flow
As dawn spreads from the east.

Birds flock round and seek to feast
On nature's generous gifts.
And slowly, surely, brightness lifts
The day, upon its settled course.
Creation praises the heavenly source.

Then swiftly, surely, with day's bright glow
Dreams fly away and realities grow.

Evelyn Balmain

JUST PASSING BY

If I wrote a poem and left it on the ground
He'd know I'd passed by without making a sound
Then he would read it and say out loud
'Someone has been and left it around
So many people pass this way
But not many of them wish they could stay
Because they dreamt of a house on the hill
Surrounded by trees.
When they were living away by the sea
The owner was a boy with long brown hair
And when she returned she found him there
Older than she dreamt
But so is she too
She walks past here now
She came and went
Trying to make out what her dream meant
So if I stare you'll understand
That the boy in my dreams is now a man
He lives in this house
Though the trees need to grow
And that's about all that you'll ever know
If I told you it all
You'd go quite red
So I think it's better left unsaid
This story is true, so please don't laugh
At this little old lady walking down the path.

Jenny Anderson

LOOK AT YOU

Look at you,
You are being strong
Starting to sort out right from wrong

Look at you,
You've been to hell and back,
Now your life is back on the track

Look at you
Looking fit and looking good
Living life the way you should

Look at you
Aiming for a better life
Not giving yourself so much strife

Look at you
You should shout out loud
Soon you will be more than a face in a crowd

Look at you
Be proud of what you do
Just love yourself and you will come through

Judi B

GROWING UP

I have watched him grow,
Seen his every move develop.
From rolling, sitting and crawling,
To screaming, standing and falling,
With dimpled hands and tiny feet,
A well-formed face with nose so neat.
But when asleep, an angel in my keep.
I cannot resist an extra little peep.
I have watched him grow, from babe in arms,
To this young lad with looks and charms.
You can talk to him and he to you,
He counts and knows his colours right through.
Where does all his vigour come from?
Dawn to dusk, he plays on and on,
'How old?' you ask, he is only three,
He really has twice the energy of me,
But when he nestles his head he lays,
To have a story told, attention he pays.
He is loving, kind, generous and gentle.
Just looking at him makes me sentimental.
I have watched him grow,
And seen his every move develop . . .

Frank E Trickett

WALK UPON BETTER BRIDGES

Always saving the best for last,
Piling up cash for a rainy day.
But the cherry rolls off your spoon onto the floor
And your money is spent, it flows away.

On the other side of the river
You spy a wonderful world,
A better life lies ahead for you.
So you decide to walk across the wooden
Bridge which spans between the glory land
And the humdrum Earth on which you dwell.
But you want to change your life.
So, gathering together all your riches
You take each new step across the bridge
To your chosen wonderland.

The bridge is rickety, woodworm-ridden
And sways as you move closer
to your nirvana.
Splinters fly in all directions as the
Bridge breaks up beneath your feet.
Your bag of riches is lost in the waters below
As you swim for your life
Towards a new life.
Is it out of your reach?
Out of your depth?
Perhaps you should have chosen to
Walk upon better bridges.

Debbie Perks

MEMORIES FOREVER

I remember so clearly
The days long ago
Our growing up years so protected and warm
The memories so clearly of those yesterdays
Where are they now, the plans and dreams made?
Schooldays so precious, of family days
Togetherness sharing a sweet misty haze
They comfort me now in the autumn of years
Our dear mother's gentleness
Holding us near
Of father who quoted us Omar Khayyám
Our childhood was happy for life then was grand
The years bringing changes as they always do
Experience knowledge the years take us to
Nothing stays as they were as time enfolds
Remembering has something we treasure and hold
So as we look back to those days that are past
The memories still clear now
Forever to last

Jeanette Gaffney

KEEPING AWAY FROM DANGER

Ring a ring of roses
Here we go Looby Loo
Don't you know how to play anymore?
Don't you know what to do?

In and out the Windows
The Farmer's in his Den
Can you only play Space Invaders
Or search the World Wide Web.

Can't you go down to the woods today
Follow the stream, go fishing
Or are you afraid you'll fall in and drown
And end up as somebody missing.

Upstairs and downstairs
In my Lady's chamber
Always play safe, surf the Net
Don't go surfing danger!

Rock a bye Baby Bunting
Cotton woolled, cocooned
Haven't you heard of hunting?
Locked in Virtual Reality
The real world is doomed.

Jan McCaffery

ENDLESS JOURNEY

The roller-coaster rides again
A new carriage has taken my place
And just to make the ride more exciting
An old discarded wagon has been resurrected
To join the train of disasters
Adding even greater danger
To this perilous journey.

The innocent novice is ensnared
I stand back and watch
Waiting for the screams of delight - then pain
The inevitable spills and thrills
Powered by attractive forces
The gravitational pull of the unknown
Until kinetic energy expires
And motion - like emotion - ceases
Empty shells are swept aside
To make way for new adventurers
Before the never-ending cycle starts again.
Clunk! - The sound of the inexorable winch
Attaching itself for the start of another nightmare
Up, up, up into the heavens - potential energy regenerated
Then the vicious switchback journey
Starts all over again, and again, and again.

Eventually - the strains and stresses will prove too much
The whole fabric will crumble and the nightmares will be no more

M J Bull

REACH YOUR GOAL

Reach your goal be brave, be bold
Forty years is not so old.
You'll be ancient when you reach your fiftieth year
So ten more years of fun: in full gear.

Your jaunty walk, your happy smile.
Bring to all a life that's worth while.
Your humour will greaten all your fun
And your glorious hair is like the sun.

Don't change your self because you're forty
Always be a little bit naughty.
Your mischievous eyes will always twinkle
As you reach your goal your grin will crinkle.

Denise Shaw

THE GREATEST GIFT

The greatest gift
Fate can bestow
No matter what the gender
It makes one's heart to glow
A cuddle is

An arm around you
A moment's balm
From our daily toil and strife
Warmth of another's palm
A cuddle is

To have someone
Embrace you tight
For a moment only you
Turns your dark into light
A cuddle is

Mary Hudson

KATH - THE LITTLE LADY WHO CARED

The birds and the squirrels huddle together as you can see,
They are all saying 'Where is our lady, where can she be?
It's winter again and no water, no crumbs, how much longer
                                    before she comes?
She never missed a day, even if she was ill she always sent
                                    someone to give us a meal,
She's not been here for ages, where is she, is she ill,?
She never neglected us before, has she left old England's shores?
So you think she's gone on before - up there to join the
                                      heavenly throng?'
They don't know like you and me, she's quite near them in
                                    the graveyard beyond,
She's done her work feeding the birds and squirrels, attending
                                        the graves,
And now she's gone, missed by some, but thought of a lot
                                    as the cold days come,
But how many others remember her solid worth, many years
                                    after she left this Earth,
Only the birds an squirrels miss her ever helping hand,
But I know 'Saint Francis' will welcome her, when she reaches
                                      the promised land.

Jan Graver-Wild

JOURNEY OF THE DYING

Understand one thing, that the journey itself is life.
Do not waste it!
Travel onwards through sadness and strife,
For every mortal pain is worth so much,
Though nothing is worth more than a loving human touch.

For I have loved.
So my life has been lived.
I have seen the beauty of nature that God does give.
I have laughed,
So I have known much pleasure
I have been given love,
That priceless treasure.
So I am not sorry to die.

I know you would follow me into the house of death
But it is I who is lost,
You have your time left.
This is my highway, this journey's not for you.
Please don't beg me to stay,
Because my life is through.
For I am not sorry to die.

You must live!
- Live on to the end.
You will feel me with you,
You can always depend.
Even from the land of the lost and the dead,
I will return to you in visions inside your head.

Now you know the reasons why
I am not sorry to die.

Kathleen Farrell

RED BLUES

No blue blood is more noble than
The Royal Blue Evertonian,
Having greater longevity,
Akin to aristocracy,
Placing our trust our reliance,
On skills known as soccer science,
It's well known I may cut you dead,
If you should mention that word Red!
Nothing more sacred or profound,
Than Goodison our hallowed ground

Our anthem's 'Never Walk Alone'
Much to the chagrin of Labone,
With all that silver on the shelf,
Our record that speaks for itself,
Anfield's the home of Liverpool,
In derbies we take them to school,
We're always there or at the top,
Thanks to great support from the Kop,
No need to argue or debate,
We are the team they love to hate!

John Smurthwaite

PRISONER OF LOVE

I long to be free
From these agonising pains
Too deep for you to feel
Crushing me with terrible pangs

> I long to be free
> From this gloom of grief
> Too dark for you to see
> Closing in like cold walls of grave

I long to be free
From these sighs and hopes shattered
Memories of abusive sprees
With which I've been battered

> Time and times I have bled
> Such that you could not see
> So many tears I have shed
> From a depth you do not know

All I needed was your love unshared
So simple for you to give
What I saw was your love in spread
So shared about, I could not receive

> Why hold me bound
> When you would not stay?
> My soul within is cast down
> Set me free I cry and pray.

Jennifer Abdulazeez

ICE MAIDEN

Encased within a tomb of ice
Expectant of the thaw
Exposed to harsh and chilling winds
Love frozen to the core

Motionless and solid
Feelings buried in the block
Merging with a landscape
Where the snowdrifts come to mock

Temperatures that plunge
To minus bitter in the night
Rising to a sharp frost
With the morning's savage bite

A maiden of the ice
She wears a blue, crisp frigid smile
A sad and lonely figure
Where sterility's the style.

Kim Montia

DREAMTIME

Earth spins
and we revolve
within the gyrating
world . . .

Morning, noon
and night
every day
every night
time for dreams
time of dreams.

I exist in
my dream dimension
far away from
the harsh reality
of life today.

The cosmic dreamscape
allows me to journey
to Mars, Venus, Saturn
and speed my way
out of the galaxy
through the pulsating
expanding
universe . . .

But where do my dreams
come from
and where do they go
after they have
absorbed me?

Stephen Gyles

'Vacancies Pour Tous' In France

Life won't be able to do what it likes
To poor rural French folk, when this summer comes.
It's been house-arrest for them, but here is release -
Just a week in the year for hardship to decrease . . .
Special days to recall on beleaguered incomes.

Through a pension's door, widows and children come
Being sure of their rooms. There are plenty to spare
On each coast of France. Hoteliers welcome their trade -
And guests take a stroll along the esplanade.
The French government, at last, makes their lives play fair.

Holiday solidarity has done its sums.
The deserving poor fill resorts by the train-load.
Frances proves to its neighbours the world holds every class,
Not just prosperous ones behind limousine glass
But members of daily bus queues up the road.

Gillian C Fisher

CHILD OF LIFE

Kingston, May 21st 1981,
Bob Marley rests, slips into purity;
Natural mystic blowing.

When he sang it,
Did he realise;
It would be his wagon,
In departures?

When he sang it,
Did he know;
The depths,
He had gone?

When he let it fly,
Did he approximate,
Its impact,
On the world;
World of hearts,
Feeling?

When he gave,
Of more,
Much more,
Did he brush,
Shock;
Feel, it was an anthem,
Of sorts?

When he did,
What he did;
Did he touch,
What he had to?

Rowland Warambwa

THE BEST THINGS IN LIFE ARE FREE

The best things in life are definitely free
And many have found this so to be:
The cheery sound of a dawn chorus filling the air
With beautiful song from everywhere;
The comfort of the sun rising majestic and round
Giving light and warmth to all around;
The pretty morning dewdrops sparkling in the sun -
Diamonds to treasure for everyone;
The daytime freshness of a gentle rain -
Cleansing and quenching the earth once again;
The glory of a garden with flowers and trees
Moving and dancing in a warm summer breeze;
The joy of a smile from someone dear,
Knowing their heart to yours is near;
The pleasure of walking along a seashore with a friend -
Not wanting the footprints to come to an end;
The delight of the countryside - fresh and green,
Offering calm and peace that's so serene;
The splendour of the hills - secure and strong -
A promise of God's love as we journey along;
The grandeur of a waterfall cascading below -
A picture of God's love that will always overflow;
The magnificence of a sunset - orange, red and gold -
A reminder of the life to come, where we'll not grow old;
The wonder of the heavens under a clear night sky,
Where Jesus Christ descended from, so He for all could die;
Just two millennia now ago, this loving act took place
And the very best thing of all in life, is God's amazing grace!

Brenda Irene Piper

A Perfect Day

This does not need much rumination
But a fable at its end it leaves
Would only tell, what an exquisite day we had,
Both together, sharing each others life with homage

Like we have for many a year
But over those years gone by, so swiftly
Which we can still look back with many a recollection
That are now a part of our treasure, that's stored deep
                                      within our hearts

Sure it did rain, but the sun shone too,
On the day that was so stupendous,
One that shall always be wished for once again
For you, are the only true love of my life

No other could ever take your place
For we, have done everything together,
Our sides are strong, showing no debility
That's what makes life a pleasure to have

So accept my card and bounty today as I do yours
For this is our wedding anniversary,
One that cannot ever be obliterated
For it was a perfect day, when we accepted each other

S J Davidson

WHEN THE ICE MELTS

The glacier starts to liquefy
Sliding down embankments
Passing obstructions the impedance of rocks
Causing an earthen dam
Curving dikes, slopes
In all directions
A shallow breakwater
Soon to be filled
With the fast and ever-flowing blue, green and
Silver gleaming water from the sea
The melted glacier
Is food to the ever-growing trees
That stand either side of the breakwater until
You meet the sea I notice as it turns
Their leaves to green how pretty and familiar those rippling
Tides this forgotten place, coming alive again
The causeway full of fishing boats
Waiting to sail once more and catch up with the tides.

Jennifer Dunkley

ANCIENT HABITAT

Upon these Isles
flowers mass in ancient hay meadow
thus our flora
come from ages past
to give sweet aroma.

Dense carpet of bluebells
canopy of beech and oak
magnificent,
yellow archangel wood daffodil
wood sorrel and wood sage
bend with enchanters nightshade and honeysuckle.

Oh beautiful purple orchid
lady's tresses par excellence
grow amid turf ancient
fancifully delicate,
to where a red-tailed bumblebee
might feed.

Oh morphos white admiral transform
that through dappled glade
purple emperor is made,
fly Adonis blue then sip of morning's dew
to navigate once more
some nectar sweet drink.

While in the hedgerows
yellowhammers sing a persistent song
ornament to spring,
blackbird brood on nursery new
aloft high nimrod passes silent
sparrowhawk mighty.

Pygmy shrew and dormouse
wait for night on hazel coppice
run red squirrel to hazelnut
scuttle through the branches,
Most magnificent red deer do rut on horizon
through sunset splendid.

Ancient habitat summer jewel
emerald with amethyst and diamond
brilliant for memory precious,
that stone cannot afford,
Sacred life song of songs.

Jeremy Jones

Awakening Call

As custodians of the world's wildlife
in terrains we've never heard
of snowy owls of arctic terns
and the brilliant humming bird.

From rainforests to the deserts
restless to discover,
creatures free to love and live
in peace with one another.

We've plundered often Mother Earth
and grown strong by selfish means,
time now to change our wills
our legacy redeem.

Small birds may disappear
if hedges we do not grow,
our gardens then we'd only share
with the starling and the crow.

The mighty ocean cannot tell
what secrets hide beneath,
but loudly echoes the seagull's cry
there are no fish to eat.

So many tribes and nations
each special and unique,
all essential to a balanced world
where strong protect the weak.

With true commitment and
respect for one another,
we the new millennium heirs
could save the world forever.

Olive Bedford

SPANISH ORANGE

Apartment blocks
and sunny skies
as I walk down the hill
an orange glimmer
before my eyes
so warm and still
like an old picture
frozen in time
now is siesta
but I cannot sleep
this quiet rustic arouses me

The distant blue
of the Spanish sea
as I walk down the hill
is calling me
a crowded beach
amongst the din
a few dark eyes
and a cheeky grin
and behind the luscious trees
on top of the hill
is a part of Spain
that belongs to me

Anna Moore

SEE THE POINT?

I cannot reach it - it is much too high,
If I do not find it - it will be 'goodbye',
Can't find the strength - or the necessary aim,
I guess that I will never attract the acclaim,
On the lower portion - I was in my stead,
Now I have to find a position - up there instead,
I need a double - I need a stiff drink,
I need some encouragement - to face the brink,
I must achieve the impossible - or I'm for the chop,
For Christ's sake come on - go into double top!

John L Wright

WISHES

Wishes in the wind
One gentle breeze,
Blowing soft:
Sends cottony seeds flying aloft

Have you ever seen
A field of green . . .
Turning shades of white
In the sunshine bright?
Waving, blowing, wishes in the wind

How many wishes did you ever blow?
When you were little, or don't you know
I know I'd pick them while walking by,
Make a wish, then blow them, and away they'd fly

How many wishes of mine have come true
So many I've lost count, how about you?

Carol Olson

STRANGE JURY!

Oh where did they dig up the jury
Did they search thro' thieves kitchens and slums
Or did they go thro' foul tenements
That house social outcasts and bums?

They find a man guilty who's only
Upholding his God-given right
To scare off pernicious offenders
The verminous gentry of night

Oh God of the just and fair-minded
Oh God of the free and the brave
They prison a man for defending his home
Against robber and crapulent knave

And with my small gift of perception
I can't see - come tell me can you
What road so-called justice is taking
In victimising the honest and true!

A Goodwin

COMPLICATED

Each day things confuse me
I sometimes have to force myself not to scream
I feel like tearing out my insides
I want to stand up and tell people what I really feel;
But I can't, I'm too scared.
Why can't people all get on?
Why must we fight and argue?
I can't cope with it all anymore.
I'm not made for this
I just want to be happy.
Why is that so much?
What is the point when we're all the same -
Equal?

Hannah Shooter

SECRET THOUGHTS

I spoke with my beloved today
It was lovely to hear his voice
To bridge the miles between us
And speak my secret thoughts.

To tell about the heartache
Whilst he is away
Of loneliness and sorrow that
Grows more and more each day.

To have his arms around me
And longing for his touch
For us to be together it
Would really mean so much.

I truly, truly love him
He is the world to me
And without him here by my side
My life is all at sea.

Diana Daley

MOTHER

The special person
The friend you need
When times are hard
And your heart breaks.
She's always there
To hear the tale
The many times
You tried and failed.
She listens patiently
As you ramble on
Offers comfort
Helps you be strong.
Giving you strength
To carry on.
Treat her tenderly
With special care
The day will come
She's no longer there.
No one else
Can take her place
You're left with memories
Of a loving face.

M Kelly

SILVER MOON

I see the shimmering silver moon
Flying in the sky
Silently your beams shine down
On us from way up high

The sun has long-since gone to bed
Her work done for the day
Now everything is quiet and still
Your rays, on Mother Earth doth play

What draws me to your magic
As you watch us through the night
A myriad stars surround you
All dancing in your light

Lying in my bed I find
I simply cannot sleep
The moon seems to be calling me
A tryst with her to keep

At last my limbs grow heavy
Freed from the chains of day
Then out into the moonlight
My spirit flies away.

Eileen Coleman

MILLY'S MAYHEM

Awoke from my nap
Around half-past four
Admire my fine whiskers
Slip out the door

Run down our lane
Yowling for Spotty
Play chase with Gerald
Fangs, Jess and Dotty

Most local folk knew us
The six cat gang
We dug up their gardens
Made trouble and sang

Ate stolen sausage
Scare dogs one, two, three
Suddenly Jess said,
'Let's race up a tree'

Paw over paw
Till all had to stop
Oh horror disaster
We got stuck at the top

They called up the firemen
To come get us down
Laughing so much
I felt like a clown

Nikky Ingram

A Wishing Well
(A sequel to 'Little Miss Muffet')

'Let us go to the well
To wish; I can tell
You would like to,' said Spider to Muffet;
'I would if I could,
I'm not sure if I should,
(If Mummy's not watching, I'd love it!)

Shall I wish for a coat
Or a horse or a boat
Or a lovely big Jaguar car?
Shall I travel the ocean? -
I haven't a notion;
Perhaps we should stay as we are!'

'Oh no!' said the spider,
'I wanted a glider,
A telly and wireless set too;
A garden with flowers
And onion-topped towers
And a room with a marvellous view!'

They wished by the well
For what - we can't tell
But they both concentrated like mad;
When they opened their eyes
They got such a surprise,
'By golly! Great Scott! We've been had!'

For nothing was there
But the fresh morning air
And the spider, Miss Muffet (and me);
They looked and they sought
For the things they had thought
But still there was nothing (but we).

'Twas a cracking good wheeze
And it's rather hard cheese
That it came to so empty an end;
But to be in good health
Is more precious than wealth
And it's daft otherwise to pretend.

Anthony Manville

What A Surprise

It was a three pound surprise,
dark-brown and crossed with a setter and a spaniel.
Each day it was a pain, hard to train and never liked its walks.
Ate like a pig and never full.
Each time my back was turned that damn dog would chew my carpets,
                      rag at my clothes and wreck the house.
Each day that dog got bigger and more hard.
People came to the house and he was ever-so nice
but when they were to leave that damn dog wouldn't let them
                              out of the door.
Everywhere I walked that dog came along, pulling and barking
                        and dragging me to the floor.
The big thing jumping around and up at me, licking and slobbering
                                  all over me.

Anne McTavish

UNCOMPETITIVE MAN

His get up and go, got up and went.
Any Chinese Chi energy has soon been well spent.

Life was such an effort, always thought through.
Gauging his stamina since he was two.

Nothing done with abandon, often gave in.
Content to watch and see someone else win.

No wish for applause for winning life's chase.
Trophies and ribbons, he could never face.

After a while, no one challenged him just to take part.
He would never win for he had no intention to start.

Saving his energy stamina in store.
Even he did not know what he was saving it for.

Let others tussle, fall to their knees.
Never a slave, like those worker bees.

To him and his sort let's raise a toast.
If life is the busy tide, he is the coast.

Life washes over him, slower yet sweeter.
In reincarnation, he could come back as a cheetah.

T A Napper

THE STRANGER
(Dedicated to the memory of Christopher (my nephew)
And all family left so bereft)

A poignant moment
As we journeyed through a secluded lane
The pain was there in its equanimity
The gathering small, heads bowed,
Flowers in abundance stood out proud
In the field that was freshly ploughed.
There will be no comforting sound of the
                        motorbike this night,
For family and friends who had come to grieve
For the young man killed in his prime.
Our hearts go out to those suffering
In the field,
For by the grace of God go I.
A trembling within my heart
Tears in my eyes.

Barbara Rose Ling

SATURN SWIMMING

Saturn swimming, smothered in a sea of contagious ecstasy
Heard it on the news today, they found it in the sea
In the deepest, deep ocean sea, a planet buried stuck
Saw it on the news today, like a moon reflected back at me
Creating anomalous gravity swells, a whole hidden other world
Like Saturn swimming, just like Saturn swimming
Floating on a sea of swirling ecstasy

Heard it on the streets today, there's a planet in the ocean
The poorest, poor paper boy, he shouts it enthusiastically
'Read it in the paper today' like an extract from a science fiction
Creating emotional modern myths, a whole elaborate tapestry
Of lies swimming, just like lies swimming
Spread upon the sea of inquisitive gossip

Saturn swimming, smothered in a sea of contagious ecstasy
It's yesterday's news today, they found out about the liars
In the darkest, dark human sea, a real myth buried stuck
It's old news today, like my past reflected back at me
Creating dangerous anxiety swells, a whole hidden unknown
Like Saturn swimming, just like Saturn swimming
Like a planet swimming, just like it see
See Saturn swimming, see it swim past me
My past it sees, it hides, Saturn swimming
Floating on the sea, an enigmatic mystery

Daryl Gilham

ROBIN AND HIS MEN OF GREEN

There was a robin looking bold
Perched on a stout bird table.
He wore a coat against the cold
Made from mink and sable.
On his head he had a hat
A polka dot sou'wester.
In the brim, there it sat
A ticket to Manchester.
A suitcase was by his side
Made from finest oak.
Now and then from inside,
There came a whimpered croak.
He checked his watch, a silver fob,
Bent down and whispered low,
Calm yourself no need to sob
It's nearly time to go.
Very soon a duck flew by
And on the robin hopped
Manchester was his cry
And in the down he flopped.

He was a showman, a raconteur,
Robin and his men of green.
Around the world they did tour
An act never had there been.
In Manchester he set his store,
Opened his rare suitcase,
Out jumped frogs galore
Dressed in crimson lace.
They hopped about like acrobats,
Then formed a perfect shape.
A model of the Empire State
Plagued by a giant ape.

They carried on, performed some more,
Moving to the robin's rhetoric.
Then the creation of Mount Rushmore,
That was their final trick.

Colin Farmer

CHANGING ROOMS

As a youth he was a daydreamer,
Often reprimanded for his lack of concentration,
He would gaze out of the schoolroom window,
His head full of wonderful images,

He helped the locals with small jobs,
Who by way of recompense,
Rewarded him with coins,
Which he hoarded,

Until the day arrived,
When his savings were sufficient,
Eagerly he visited the decorators,
Purchasing assorted paints,

As time passed he became quite proficient,
People asked for his services,
And his talent did not go unnoticed,
By word of mouth news of his skill spread,

A visitor came to see him,
Offering an important commission,
A contract was drawn up immediately,
The Creation Of Adam was to be brought to life,

He worked tirelessly day and night,
The eager young man's dreams,
Becoming a reality,
The painting of The Last Judgement a legacy,

And so the scenes unfolded,
Meticulously his visions,
Were detailed overhead,
Days turned into years,

Time marched on and took its toll,
His neck and back gave him pain,
Some days his hands,
Could scarcely clutch the brush,

This obsession led to a lifetime achievement,
A superb fresco unsurpassed,
The Sistine Chapel, Michaelangelo, the artist,
Changing rooms sixteenth century style.

Ann G Wallace

FROG IN THE THROAT

So the story goes,
Many, many years ago,
A citizen of Brussels,
Suffered with the snuffle.
Suffered with it from birth;
Only slight at first,
As they got older, the snuffle got worse.

On their fourth birthday,
Washday, rainy Wednesday.
Had a terrible coughing attack.
Did not work, good slap on the back.
Without doubt.
The world's worse coughing bout.
That almost polished him out.

Tried to cure
The cough, a helpful witch.
She got him to swallow some manure
Looking stuff, which did not cure.
The bitch,
Dangled a frog on a stretch of thread
Down the citizen's throat, put him to bed.

In the night the frog wriggled about.
At the back of the throat.
The thread broke.
The citizen awoke with a frog-like croak.
That's how came about,
The saying, 'Have a frog
In one's throat'.

B G Clarke

Magnolia Lament

It was proffered with such grace.
One tight solitary bloom
cupped within protective shield
of green and with a strange
perfume I could not place.
This wax-like sculpture
I held with awe, aware
that I had never seen before
a Magnolia flower at so close a range.

Within my room I placed it
reverently in china bowl and,
when next I looked, within the hour
its petals had unfolded to reveal
a secret chamber from its waxen seal.

I dreamt that night of caverns
filled with jewels and little pools
where angels played:
but come the morn the beauty
of my bloom had wilted from
its creamy wax-like form
to one of parchment brown.

With sorrow I surveyed
the mound of petals,
so majestic yesterday,
now collapsed upon themselves
in wretched disarray:
and pondered how it came to pass
that so mature a tree
could bear a bloom so beauteous
to last but for a day.

Pat Holton

A Poet's Fareweill Tae Ye Bonnie Lass

Tho I'd vou'd tae write ye verse nae mair
Wi ye haen hurt ma, O sae sair!
O bonnie lass wi smilin face an glintin een
Ma hert's still alowe wi luve for thee.

This sal be ma vera lest . . .
Tho it's nae the ane I aince thocht o'gien ye lass
For it wad have been a myth . . .
An aa I've ivver said aboot ye, wis aye the truith!

I think aften o' that day an time
Whan ye tore at ma sowl tae lay it bare
Wi sic cauld, cauld shouther an quaitness o' the lair;
O! haen ye jist pit yer wee saft haun in mine
It wid have been Elysium Divine
But na, it wisna tae be
An noo, hou I curse thae fey lines!

In nae wey did I dismensefu ettle tae be
Or desairve sic displeisure as shawn by thee
That ye've broken ma hert . . . I canna forsey
For I nou sit alane, an O lassie hou I dae cry . . .
The tears thae stream doon ma cheeks intae ma mou
Aa through writin a luve poem tae you.

The pain lies heavy wi'in ma briest
Fur frae furst tae hinmaist, a wrote jist wurds o' praise.
At aa time through yer tender an growin year
Ma luve an fondness wiz aye sincere
An wha but me wiz aye near in joy or sorrow?
As I sit an greet the russet beech leaves fa
An I feel as lanely as the ae Flanders poppy that grows on Lillyla
Ma tears thae mak ma paper sodden
O wae's me, wae's me, ye hae truly been ma Flodden.

Gilbert

SNAP

I hunted and hunted and hunted in vain
For an 'off the peg' evening dress, really quite plain.
Just as it seemed there was nought for me made,
I spotted it, Grecian, and trimmed with gold braid.

As hostess that night, hubby's boss to impress
It behoved me, I thought, not to settle for less.
A white chiffon dream, although heavy the cost
If it helped his promotion all was not lost!

Evening approached, I was ready to slay,
Dinner was cooked - all under way,
Footsteps were heard, I answered the door
Coats were collected, surprise was in store!

There stood my lady in very same gown!
My fury was mounting, I tried not to frown!
She saved the day by a well-humoured, 'Snap!'
Then very discreetly slipped into her wrap!

Lola Perks-Hartnell

THE MAGIC SHOE

There once was a little mouse who lived in a shoe,
but she had lots of things to do.

This shoe was a very particular kind and so is
my story as you will find.

The side of the shoe was a moving floor and at
the end of it was a little door.

Whenever the little mouse wanted to go out, she
just had to give a little shout.

Up came a spider straight away and suddenly
the floor began to sway.

The spider was the mouse's guide, he often took
her for a ride.

After a little while they would stop and get out
at the grocer's shop.

The beetle inside was always polite, whenever
the little mouse came in sight.

The very best cheese he always sold her, as he
looked at the spider over his shoulder.

No webs today he seemed to say and the
little mouse began to pay.

Out of the shop then they would go, to the
grasshopper's house at the end of the row.

In shiny suit he waited there, always ready
to greet the pair.

Then the three sat down to tea and all told stories full of glee.

Suddenly the spider looked at the clock and they got an awful shock.

So along the path they made their way, they must be home at the end of the day.

Then once again the little guide, took his mouse friend for a ride.

Soon she was safely back in her shoe, so the spider had nothing more to do.

Margaret T Emmerson

RAINBOW

fishing -
- -
plip! - - - ripple - - - - - - - - - - - - - - - - -
- -
fishing -
- -
plomp! - - - big ripples - - - - - - - - - - - -
- -
fishing -
- -
a touch - a nibble - *strike!*
a screeching reel - a plunging line -
a fighting back to make him mine -
a bowing rod - a straining wrist -
an inching in of plunge and twist -
a wearing down of strength and will -
a duel to death of wit and skill -
- -
molten silver in the net
shimmers as it arches yet
- -
on fresh green grass in basket lain -
A rainbow trout in battle slain
- -
fishing -
- -
plip! - - - ripple - - - - - - - - - - - - - - - - -
- -
fishing -
- -

Edward Fursdon

SHEHEREZADE

Sheherezade's mellifluous tongue
Dripped honeyed words, spoken and sung.
For a thousand and one nights her tales were told,
She talked and talked till the moon was old.
Tales of love and tales of hate,
Tales of people who couldn't wait.
Old folk, young folk, anyone at all,
She held her listeners in her thrall.
She spoke of treasures and jewels untold,
Of silver coins and bars of gold.
Stars in the heavens and flowers on earth,
She spoke of death, and she spoke of birth.
Smiles and frowns, laughter and tears,
Old people's worries and young folk's fears.
Animals, people, angels, a child,
Emotions that range from gentle to mild.
The Emir succumbed and granted her life,
Feared time without her and made her his wife.

Denise Marriott

NIGHT FEAR

The night owl screeched, its flight path disturbed as it silently foraged.
The moonlight filtered through the bare branches of the ancient oaks.
Who was abroad? What was their purpose?
Rustlings in the undergrowth marked their passing,
Casting no shadows, this way or that,
A sudden chill wind whipping paths through the trees.
The night creatures listened, holding their breath,
For abroad in the wood, silent and searching,
Was one who was watching, awaiting a sound
Or a movement, to know where they were.
A life to be taken - a family to feed.
A deep fear had fallen, would they be the one
The poacher had come for, invading their home.
The nightjar raised its voice, calling a warning.
Birds rose from the trees, their feathers a-trembling,
Attracting the attention of he who was searching,
Allowing the others to make their escape
Into holes, into burrows, through old tracks and pathways.
Tonight would yield nothing. The daylight would come.
Every creature had found its way home.

Vara Humphreys

Lament From The Aquarium

I was sent to boarding school in the Autumn of nineteen fifty-three -
a tiny minnow who'd never set fin in a vast and roiling sea.
'We're sending you there in the hope it makes a man of you,'
                                                                                   Father claimed;
and little I knew of the sharks that basked, just waiting to tear
                                                                                   and maim.
I joined the shoal, but fish out of water are always shunned by the rest;
and sharp-toothed bullies had singled me out, though I tried my
                                                                                 minnow's best.
to skim or dive and hide in the rocks of learning, of language and art;
and took refuge in the pearlescent shells of literature's
                                                                                 dream-filled heart.

But sharks are relentless; the scent of fear will draw killers to their food.
They dine on defenceless flesh; they relish the tasting of tears
                                                                                 and blood.
They hound to exhaustion a victim; then, remorseless, seek further prey.
And while larger shoals swam out of their reach, and darted out of
                                                                                 their way,
I could not escape. They ripped out my mind. They took pleasure in
                                                                                   my fear;
till my fins and tail seized up, and I was found floating under the pier -
face-up on the water with staring eyes, and my senses all but gone.
Now I drift through weed, and talk to snails - in my silent aquarium.

J M Service

FACTION FIGHTERS

With blood curdling cries
and sticks flaying on high,
wheeled round defiantly
and drawing attention sly,
from persons intrigued
and stunned passers-by.

A realistic display
of traditions so bold,
pantomimical endeavour
begins story to unfold.
Customs outlawed by clergy
and aristocrats alike - old,
a sport to deny - yet retold.

As a living history - true
street theatre re-enactions,
reviving - as was before
as common place distractions.
Fighting or sport,
by defined local factions.
All in period costume and brogue,
A story to enrapture - as vogue.

Gary J Finlay

FACTS OR FICTION 2000

The young generation, find today,
They are being driven, in many ways.
In our bedroom, we shed many a tear,
Our parents arguing, we can hear.
From a child, we feel our life is in vain,
To leave home, is our aim.
Our father's domineering voice, we can hear,
The shrieks from our mother, given in fear.
Came that day, we find a purpose in our life,
Able to afford, a motor car, or bike.
With no goodbyes we drive away,
And speed along, some motorway.
That speed we find, gives us a thrill,
Unaware, that speed can kill.
If an untimely end, becomes our fate,
Has our parent's actions bred our hate,
Or will our parents love, come too late . . .

Brian Marshall

LOVE IN THE FOREST

At the stream, with ears alert she lapped her fill,
Slowly raising her head, she then stood quite still.

She had left the forest for a special reason,
A beautiful full grown tigress now in season.

Her scent had been sprayed on tree and bush,
Around this forest glade with grass so lush.

Green eyes surveyed the tree line, searching, alert,
Where was this male with whom she was ready to flirt?

Round and round she prowled, head erect she listened.
While the morning dew like jewels on the grass glistened.

The air was filled with a raucous sound as she purred,
At last the long awaited growl of the male was heard.

Down on the grass she lay with a twitching tail,
Patiently waiting for her selected male.

Suddenly it happened, one to the left and one to the right,
For her favours they would each test their strength and fight.

They entered the clearing each with head lowered to the ground,
They eyed each other, growling and walking warily around.

Vicious was the next scene, nature's battle in the raw,
Each contestant becoming scarred with tooth and claw.

Victor and vanquished had given their very all,
More's the pity that in the end one had to fall.

A new contestant entered the arena to join in the affray,
The victor and the vanquished turned and moved cautiously away.

The newcomer had won his bride without striking a blow,
To his newly found partner he was her conquering hero.

The next few days they spent as they wished,
Each enjoying their short nuptial tryst.

Nature's climax would be over in a couple of days,
Then back to the forest, each taking different ways.

F Hirst

ESCAPE

The raindrops patter on my window
Echoing round my tiny room.
I sit here in my wretchedness,
Sad
Alone
Rejected.
Escape,
Let me escape.

Looking out through invisible bars
From eyes veiled in tears
I feel the cold sun
Throwing out its rays of ice.
I draw backwards into misery
Pained by a tortured soul
Tormented from my thoughts within.

Free,
Let me go free.
I seek out the little green bottle
It weeps for me.
I drink of its non-existence
Then lean back into Nirvana.

Now my body still sits here
Yet I have escaped.

David Brownley

WHEN THE WIND BLOWS

Now Adam has his problems.
Number One. Speaks out of turn.
Yet worry not the chance will be
Your ears will ever burn!
  For if he has a word to say,
  He will boast it loud and clear.
  At times I wish the floor would
  Open up . . . So I could disappear!
He never means to cause offence,
But does . . . he can't hold back!
Wit he has a-plenty . . .
It's just diplomacy he lacks.
  It's hard for me to shut him up,
  As he's faster than a colt!
  And when that look comes in his eye,
  To the door I want to bolt!
I died a death the other day
Whilst visiting our Nellie;
She suffers trapped wind - (so embarrassing) -
When gas blows - up her belly.
  Now Adam sat as good as gold,
  But soon 'mi laddo' shone . . .
  For wind she broke . . . and out he spoke
  - 'I'll name that tune in one!'

Linda Zulaica

THE STORY OF MY LIFE!

Oh no! Something small and fluffy
mashed beyond recognition.
Mortality high on this stretch. Get a move on!
Same old fart in the pork-pie hat
dragging his fuming crocodile with him,
belching diesel scented steam
to hang in the saturated air about the junction.
Cold. Autumnal. Wet leaves on the line.
Prat in a red XR2 should show about now.
Always hear him a mile before I see him.
There he goes. Two wheels on the pavement,
burning oil, doubtful MOT, insurance,
Guinness label on the dash. Always on the dash.
Where does he think he's going!
Damn the stupid boy.
Water in the hollow. Gathers there.
Bet it was a pool with ducks
in a less time conscious age.
Lights out again. Early morning chicken.
No! Not another. Hedgehog this time.
Never the brain dead kids from the comp,
who think it's cool to swagger in the road,
dawdle with the air of, 'Touch me if you dare'.
Little b*****ds. Do their parents know, care.
Well, you stupid sod!
No wonder the wing's gone.
Taxis, buses and third party nutters,
the knackered hot-hatch,
little old ladies who cling to the gutters.
Turning right.
Bet you ninepence the Merc is in the wrong lane.
Told you! B*****d!
'And now, the hottest sound around,
on both sides of the Atlantic . . .'
It must be OK for bread vans to block the road
as long as they are on the pavement

on double yellow lines, hazard warnings
blinking in the fog.
And here we are, bosses son in my space.
So begins another working day.

John Tirebuck

Nature's Curse

We were wrenched from the farm
Like a proud tree, torn out of the earth
Blown by savage winds
Leaving unseen roots helplessly exposed
Just how Mama says she feels
Ashamed at her unexpected nakedness
Da almost lost his reasoning
Scratching at the dirt
Forced to be an onlooker in nature's fickle game
He watched his crops
And his young ones rise
Then fall in parched silence
Feasting their swollen bellies
On worthless dust
We were born to this land
And toiled as willing slaves
Sustaining its thirst with our sweat
Harnessing every reckless, changing mood
Of new generations
But now, stunned at its uselessness
We are orphaned by death
Solemn and bewildered we left
This place that had given and taken
Will become a legacy for familiar
Wandering ghosts
Rocking and swaying in our worn out truck
Creeping like a giant snail
Chomping up the highway
Reaching farther and farther into tomorrow
We five, hungry for one more chance.

H W Fleming

THE TESTIMONIAL MATCH

They've signed a new striker, so he has to go!
His age is against him, its starting to show.
He's made some mistakes, he's the first to admit.
That it's time to move on, now his face doesn't fit!

He was part of the 'team' for a number of years,
He's tasted the glory and also the tears!
His 'fans' used to love him and sing out his name,
But time waits for no man, now things aren't the same.

He shared a great partnership with a colleague,
They 'scored' many times, they won cups and the league!
But lately its soured and they've won sweet FA,
Now the magic has gone and it shows in their play!

He's been substituted, he's not up to scratch,
But they've granted him a testimonial match.
They claim in the 'best interests' of the team,
He should go, for the sake of his own self-esteem!

But he's given his heart and his soul, blood and sweat!
All they shared, he knows will be so hard to forget.
But his lawyers assure him, to quit while ahead,
Is much better than flogging a horse that is dead!

Now the 'contract' is torn up, he no longer plays,
Except with his children, on his 'access' days!
His former team-mate has found another source,
Of provider, beside her, since they've been 'divorced'!

He was part of the team for a number of years,
But now there's just silence instead of the 'cheers'.
Now he's hung up his boots, all he kicks is his heels!
Its a funny old game' - these surprises love deals!

Roger Carpenter

SUMMER IDYLL

The hills and the trees, birds and breeze
And the pollen giving me a colossal sneeze
The sun and the clouds, moor and sea
The buzzing insect which fell in my tea
Dip of the bough and wave of the corn
Sheep looking smaller when newly shorn
Sights and sounds from far and near
The dog waving its tail round my ear
Damp of the grass and cramp in my knee
Wasp round the ham and the questing bee
While a caterpillar examined food on my plate
Ants whizzed round at a frantic rate
Buttercup, daisy and threat of a shower
So the picnic was nice though only lasting an hour

G D C Stribling

LIZA JANE

Knock, knock on the door broke the silence of the night,
The little man stood waiting as he saw a flash of light.
Inside the woman trembled, as she wrestled with the door,
Stepping over her drunken husband laying on the floor.
'Come in Doctor, this way please,' the nervous woman said,
He followed her to a room where a girl lay on the bed.
'It's Liza Jane,' the woman pointed. 'Hello,' the Doctor replied,
As he sat down on the bed, Liza looked terrified!
'What's the matter my pretty, my lovely Liza Jane?
But she wouldn't answer him, just pointed to the pain.
The Doctor examined her and was appalled by what he saw,
Her body was covered with bruises and she was only four.
'I think it's her appendix. It's bad,' the Doctor said,
'I'll take her to hospital myself and get her in a bed.'
He wrapped her up and took her from that God-forsaken house,
The Doctor had been suspicious before, that her father was a louse.
He would never have forgiven himself, if lovely Liza Jane
had been *dead* the next time he called on her again.
Liza made a good recovery and was placed in foster care,
Where she'll get love and tenderness, that to her was so rare.
She no longer has to suffer, no longer has to fear,
Only childhood accidents and happiness will make her shed a tear.
Her parents were prosecuted, as both committed the crime
And the judge told them that they would serve a lengthy time.
It will take a long time for Liza Jane to forget
And for those brutal parents, she'll spare no time to fret.

Ria Telford

WORK EXPERIENCE

Working here at the estate agents
Working hard each day
I really feel it's a pity
they can't offer me some pay

I'm a very dedicated person
and thorough in all I do
Do you think if I stay long enough
money will filter through

All the staff are friendly
and the photocopier my best friend
Producing all the details
that never seem to end

I came here for a fortnight
for work experience they say
Well, it's been over twelve weeks now
and I'm desperate for some pay

Jobs are hard to come by
Work experience does the trick
It will give the employer a good idea
if you are in good nick

Time is ticking over
and still I have no job
Do you think that I should tell them they should
stuff the blinking lot!

June Slater

THE SPIRITS DANCED AT MIDNIGHT

The spirits danced at midnight - at the striking of the clock
In the moonlit winter churchyard, that lies beside the Lock.
There was Ted from 1864 and Nineteenth Century Dan;
Young Lil the WAF from World War Two - and gentle little Fran.
And Connor, from the Emerald Isle played Airs upon his Pipe
as in and out, and round about, they danced each winter's night.
It had been Mother Brown's idea - to dance their deaths away;
She'd always loved a knees-up when she'd lived (down Camden way)
And George, the Butler (1910) chose Lady Anne to dance;
he'd always fancied her in life - in death, he stood a chance!
And so they did the Jitterbug, the Waltz, and Highland Fling
the Charleston, Jive and Irish Reel - and everyone would sing.
They were a pretty noisy bunch, but no one heard or saw,
for with the dawning of the day, they were in their graves once more.

Until, one night the stranger came - a man of quiet Grace
and watched them from the Graveyard's edge; He had a lovely face.
And George the Butler saw him first, and fell on Mother Brown
who cannoned into Dan and Ted - and everyone fell down!
And Connor ceased his piping, all was quiet, till little Fran
said: 'Look all of you! - He sees us; He's a very Special Man.'

The stranger smiled, and in a very gentle voice He said:
'What are you all still doing in this Garden of the dead?
I came that you might have new life
I came to set you free. One day you'll have new bodies -
But till then - will you come with Me?'
So, one by one, they followed, for something about His face
told them that He was someone from a Very Special Place.
And the Spirits who'd danced at Midnight, were suddenly hushed
                                                           and still.
No one had ever seen them dance . . .
Now nobody ever will.

Faith Honeysett

INSTINCT OF A PET COLLIE DOG

A noble breed, the collie dog,
And companion of man's ease.
Master supreme of the labour he loves,
Enjoying his master to please.
What wonderful inner instinct
Warns this animal, bred in a town,
That the ewe, almost in lamb,
Must be left and let to lie down?
The flock rounded out of the field
By the skill of the farmer's man,
Leave their weary sister behind them,
To manage as well as she can.
But, lest he should forget her,
And leave her behind to her fate,
The collie insistently warns him,
Before he can shut the great gate,
And standing alert and on guard,
Till the creature her breath has regained,
The sentinel watches the straggler,
Till her place in the flock is maintained.

Elizabeth Wynne

Dandy Jack The Highwayman

Dandy Jack was a highwayman during the eighteenth century,
He held up the coaches of the rich and landed gentry.
Relieving them of their money and jewels,
Then shoot his pistols into the air to warn any resisting fools.
Robbing the London to Rochester, Gravesend to Rochester stages,
You would never have found Dandy Jack working for honest wages.
For about ten years he carried out his villainous trade,
Some said with the devil, a pact he had made.
Always mounted on his favourite grey mare,
At the chance of being apprehended he did not care.
In the local taverns and inns they would sing rousing songs,
Making of him a hero, in spite of his evil wrongs.
Then one day he went too far in his wrong doing,
Which eventually led to the highwayman's ruin.
At the Shorne and Cobham cross-roads he did rob a
Stage coach and commit foul murder,
When the victim's wife protested he pretended
He had not heard her.
The slain man's friends devised a clever plan
And vowed to get the dastardly highwayman.
The brave men did not have long to wait,
Near Chalk Church on the Rochester Road the brazen robber
Took the bait.
From behind a tree he rode out calling 'Stand and deliver,'
And for his trouble was shot twice in the
Head and once through the liver.
On moonlit nights his ghostly apparition is often observed,
Galloping by without a word.
With flaming fire coming from his horse's hooves,
Dandy Jack is still trying to carry on his daring do's.

Bardon

The Last Of His Kind

It was a dreary day in more than one way and under a bruise-laden sky,
From a cavern underground came a terrible sound that reverberated on high,
A dragon appeared and though he was feared, he was regarded with an air of awe
And all poor souls did shake at the noise he did make when he rendered his mighty roar.

He was the last of his kind of sound body and mind, though ancient from tail tip to snout
And what he didn't know about life's ebb and flow wasn't worth worrying about,
He had seen lands rise and fall, some mighty, some small and seen islands swallowed by the sea,
He had seen mysteries unravelled for far he had travelled much farther than you or than me.

He was awoken this day by a knight, Sir L' Ray, who had searched for his nemesis,
And the knight held a grudge 'cos of the sweet Lady Rudge who he could only awake with a kiss,
For his embrace to ignite and lessen his plight he needed a crimson flood,
No mere mortals vein could ease love's cruel pain only dragon 'type O' scaly blood!

The knight had his name but he thought it a shame to destroy such a magical beast,
So with the aid of a witch when sky was as pitch, they used a sleep spell stole from a priest
The magic was cast and into the past the dragon's legend fell,
The blood safe to take for naught could awake 'the last of his kind' from the spell.

Twelve centuries of sleep ten fathoms deep, the earth and the grass help to hide, the dragon in lair - legends point where? To a vast Welsh mountain side,
So if you're at play and you notice some day that the slope you are stood on doth shake,
Run as fast as you can! Warn all mortal man! That the dragon with vengeance awakes!

Bronwyn Lewis

PRETENDERS

Eleven clones posed and pranced like prize fighters;
luminous boiler suits studded with rhinestones,
reclaimed black hair shaped and trimmed like topiary,
chests menaced by medallions, rings like gold warts.
I wore a sober suit and tie, honest grey hair:
but two years previously the world had been lost
amid a maze of grief following news of my sudden death!

There were four performances of American Trilogy,
two interpretations of Jailhouse Rock,
versions of Heartbreak Hotel, Blue Suede Shoes,
It's Now Or Never, Are You Lonesome Tonight.
After I finished Crying In The Chapel
I bowed to a stunned silence
until almost deafened by an avalanche of applause;
while the final contestant stumbled through Love Me Tender.

Contestant number four who had performed American Trilogy
was thrilled with third place,
contestant number nine with his version of Heartbreak Hotel
was disappointed to have finished second.
After someone tapped me on the shoulder
I turned around and gazed at contestant number two
who had sung It's Now Or Never
one knee at the front of the stage
mopping his brow with each pair of knickers thrust at him

I smiled realising I was still loved
but relieved it was more dead than alive.

Stephen Atkinson

SEA DOG'S SEED BED

A sea dog of wit from St Briavels
Conversed all his life on two levels.
'Sink me funeral boat
In a field sown wi' oat
'Cos I'll likely get wild wi' she-devils.'

Frederick Poole

STARS AND SPIKES

Spiky is a hedgehog and a tiny one at that!
He longs to grow and grow and grow
To reach up . . . to the stars
Each night he gazes up at them . . . a twinkle in the sky
They seem to wink and smile at him
Spiky . . . catch us if you can
And sure enough as time goes by
Our Spiky . . . really grows
But only round his middle
He's now a roly poly ball.
Soon his home is far too small
And a new one he must find
As he nestles deep in leaves and moss
To sleep the winter months . . . away
Till springs new life and lighter days
Awakens our prickly friend
Who stretches out, to uncoil his paws
From around his sleepy head.
It's then he looks, it's then he sees
He's grown bigger than by far
But is he big enough to touch a star, within his paw?
As night time falls, he gazes up and up and up some more!
Until he sees those stars have moved
From when they were before
But never mind our Spiky thinks
Two can play that game
And I will reach those stars . . . one day!
I know I really will,
For I've seen them shining, brightly
In the homes of . . . my human friends!

Penwork 2000

DESERTED FRIEND

Your empty chair confirms you've gone away -
how can I live, without you all is dull.
Who are you with, to flirt with day by day?

I'll take your cushion in as clouds are grey,
lent books abandoned, hurt my feelings still.
Your empty chair confirms you're still away.

I'll wear your hat - although the sun won't play.
Your vacant seat teases my aching soul.
Who are you with, to flirt with day by day?

You did not write my sorrow to allay.
Who's your new friend upon whom you can call?
Your empty chair confirms you've gone away.

There's no more peace within my gardening day.
I try to leave - be more original.
Who are you with, to flirt with day by day?

I'm still bereaved, outside I cannot stay.
Downcast I look, my swollen eyes are full.
Your empty chair confirms you've gone away -
So, who're you with, to flirt with day by day?

Geraldine Bruce

AN AGE OF GOLD

Fifty is an age of gold
With half a century now told.
Before the autumn of our years
Mid-summer precious gold appears.

Now passed the spring when life began
Embarking on the age of man.
Trials of childhood, joy of youth
Left behind the age uncouth.

Battle for loves won and lost,
On life's ocean being tossed.
In summerhood of life there's gain
From understanding of the pain.

Summer colours vibrant shine
Taste the rich of summer vine.
While in gold summer, preserve your store
Of memories - time will endure.

Anita Richards

Young MacDonald's Farm

Young MacDonald has a farm where oats and barley grow,
she also keeps some animals - e i e i o.
None are sent to market, nor used to work or hunt,
they're her pets, including Big Fat Pig and Grunt the Runt.

And on the farm is the brown cow who's chewing on her cud
while watching Big Pig and the runt rolling in the mud.
The old grey mare is also there, plus a black dog named Blue,
free range chickens roam around, and a rooster too.

They all live in harmony on MacDonald's farm
where things are grown organically, not causing any harm.

One night something terrible did happen on the farm,
Big Pig was grabbed from his pen and hurled into a car.
The pig-thief laughed and shouted 'You'll make lovely bacon!'
Big Pig was so terrified that he started shakin'.

Back on the farm there was a fuss, when the brown cow mooed,
the black dog, Blue, growled and barked and the cock-a-doodled dooed.

Young MacDonald ran to see what was going on,
she went into the barn and found both her pigs were gone.
Sitting down, head in her hands, she was filled with grief,
but didn't know that Grunt the Runt had followed the pig-thief.

In the dark the little pig planned the great escape,
when the car stopped, the thief got out to open up the gate,
Grunt jumped up into the car and with his little snout,
pushed and pushed and pushed until Big Pig was pushed out!

Off they ran back to their home on MacDonald's farm,
where she welcomed both of them with wide, open arms.
Everything's now safe and sound on MacDonald's farm,
because she has just fitted a security alarm.

Margaret Richer

SHADOWS OF THE NIGHT

The sun sinks slowly down to die,
and the evening shadows fall.
And in the dusk a lonely cry
alerts the hunted one and all.

Birds in the lower branches roost,
as the leaves tremble in the breeze.
Night time shadows like a ghost,
comes to flit among the trees.

Is that the call of the lonely owl,
as it searches for its prey?
Hooting its call while on the prowl,
that was hidden during the day.

In the night there is another sound,
it's like the beating of a heart,
stampeding feet upon the ground
as the hunted ones depart.

The moonlight casts an eerie glow,
and bathes the scene in light.
Until the dawning sun does show,
the moon commands the night.

V C Gregory

A Knight In A Raincoat

A swirling and sibilant strident wet night
Lashed through city streets roaring wildly with great
Bursts of rain. Buttoned-up hooded well we strode on
Down grey narrow pavements towards the bright lights
Of a road-crossing. There with the splashing of cars
Speeding by, we all waited for our turn to cross.
A bunch of wet people just waiting for dry
Sheltered calm in the underground station nearby.

At last the lights changed but I waited a moment
As youngsters dashed speedily in a large mob,
Then came a grey shadow, a strong hand on my shoulder,
Such a tall man beside me was making a space
For me to proceed. Safely there I looked up.
His face was familiar. In seconds he'd gone.
I knew who he was - but had not thought to meet
A raincoated Cardinal in a wet London street.

Margaret Connolly

RUNNING THE GAUNTLET

An embarrassing incident occurred to me,
When visiting friends in a garrison city.
To the park we went, with shouts full of glee,
To use the playground, my two boys and me.

Hot, humid air soon made me aware
The boys couldn't take any more.
The baths were so near, I had an idea . . .
A cool bath! - So went through the men's door.

So, refreshed and clean, they dashed to the scene
Of joy on the swings so near . . .
With no one around, I quickly dis-gowned
To soak, and enjoy without fear.

Without any onus - oh what a bonus -
Suddenly: yelling and clatters galore . . .
With horror, I realised, that I was penalised
In the gent's! 'Oh, please, lock; hold the door!'

I hurriedly dressed and trembling with fear,
I silently waited - until noise abated,
Then crept out, expecting 'all clear',
Twelve steps to walk (which I couldn't baulk)
Where a whole regiment smilingly waited . . .

With legs all a-tremble I tried to assemble
My dignity, passing those men.
Soft wolf whistles, winks, they showed their approval,
When they saw the reason, for their 'now removal'.

Never again! I declare - will I ever share
A men's only utility thing!
I don't want attention, (so don't think I'll mention,)
My indiscreet, unacceptable; fling!

Ivy Cawood

The Duel

The house stood alone on the dark moor,
steeped in history, we started our tour.
Through the entrance, which loomed so high,
we gazed around with an interested eye.

Walking through rooms we followed our guide
who imparted his knowledge with so much pride.
Portraits of ancestors adorned the great hall,
where ladies in crinolines danced at many a ball.

Intrigues were rife with affairs of the heart,
secret love triangles which all played a part.
All was destroyed, that day at dawn
when brother fought brother until death on the lawn.

I lingered alone to gaze around,
the rest walked on until there was no sound.
My thoughts were mixed not a word could I say
but I knew in my heart that I belonged here today.

Drawn to the staircase with all its splendour
I saw her before me, her face so warm and tender.
The glitter of jewels, the rustle of her gown,
my senses were swimming, I thought I would drown.

Coming toward me, with a smile on her face
her head held high, she had such poise and grace.
My eyes held hers, suddenly I could see
the face before me, was a picture of me.

Carole Hoy

Sam

Today we went to the RSPCA
To look at the puppies, that had been thrown away,
On a lay-by we found him, is what she said,
We picked him up and gave him a bed.

She opened the cage, you came bounding out,
Jumping and diving, all about.
You came to me and then to Pete,
You had a lovely soft coat and four white feet.

This is the one, we will love at our home,
If nobody claims him, could we take him home.
A week she said, it seems a long time,
But in seven days, I know you'll be mine.

February the 27th, was that special day,
Paid sixty quid and lead you away.
In our family home, you'll be loved and thrive,
Were a family of four, but now we're five.

We'll love you and care for you, and take you for walks.
A name we have yet, had no time for talks.
'Sam' was the name we pulled out the hat,
We shouted your name, you seemed to like that.

We'll give you a bed and something to eat,
After your feast, you lay at my feet.
I love you Sam, I said to you,
You looked up at me as if to say 'I love you too.'

Our family's complete, until this day,
Well worth a trip to the RSPCA.

Mandy Craven

The Old Bucket

It stood in the dairy, clean and shiny bright,
Pretty coloured label still stuck on tight.
A big hand grabbed it and carried it away
Down to the milking shed to stand in the hay.
Up again and plonked between a cow's great legs.
Back to the dairy, and emptied down to dregs.
Not shiny now, and the label came unstuck.
It was dropped, and kicked, and fell into the muck.
Washed again and clean but with a great big dent,
Now it didn't stand up straight at all, it leant!
Banished to the calf-shed it was kicked some more,
Ending up quite battered outside the cow-shed door.
Then on its side it was visited by snails,
Who left it covered in tiny silver trails.
Every week when the rubbish men came near
It lay, still, in the grass, trembling with fear.
Then it got so wet its bottom rusted through.
The farmer's wife came by - 'Ah! this one will do.'
Picked it up, and looked at it, and off she went.
With a block of wood she hammered out the dent,
Set to with paint brush and when she'd stopped her toil,
Filled it up with stones and lots of lovely soil.
When the rubbish is collected every single week
The bucket stands its ground without so much a squeak,
Knowing that it's safe from collection and the 'tip'.
With all its leaves and flowers, and bamboo stick,
It stands, by the kitchen door, all shiny red,
It isn't an old bucket now, but a flowerpot instead!

Haidee Williams

THE LIGHTHOUSE

God's word is like a lighthouse
Warning travellers upon the narrow road
Of the dangers along the way,

Keep the beacon light always in sight
And you will arrive safely
At the Kingdom of God's Earthly Paradise
And live eternally.

Norman Mason

CHILD OF MINE AND CHILD OF YOURS

Child inside you
Needs to speak
Find a voice
Time to weep

Child within you
Needs to know
Time for answers
Time to sow

Child long silent
Needs to talk
Time to bear it
Not to walk

Child you're still there
Eyes so dim
Time to find out
Reach for him

Child forgetting
Time to wake
Time for stopping
It's not too late

Child I promise
You'll be sane
Time to reconcile
Years of pain.

Wynne Stearns

PICKING UP THE PIECES

Out of the taxi she stumbled,
leaving her bag and keys behind,
you can't let me in beauty she mumbled,
the dog walked off and whined.

Curled up small upon the step,
shivering with the cold,
when she turned back I leapt
and then the black eye was bold.

Too much to drink this Saturday night
and all memories of it were lost,
when she cried I held her tight,
all she asked was how much did the taxi cost.

Holding her purse so very tight,
she kept mumbling I fell,
maybe she's been in a fight,
is she lying I never could tell.

Donna Marie Smart

Mick's Story

This is the tale that's told by Mick
'Twill make you laugh or make you sick
Depends on how you look at life
Whether it's happy or full of strife

It begins with Mick on his motor bike
Speeding along, all peaceful like
With never a worry and never a care
He suddenly found himself in the air
Right over the top of a car he'd hit
He sailed quite high, on his head he lit
Damaged his knee caps and cracked his skull
As he lay in the roadway feeling dull
A friend of his mother's came walking by
Mick felt as if he were going to die
But she looked at him with a vacant gaze
'Hello Mick,' she said. 'How's your mother these days?'

Betsy Van Warmer

MAGICAL MYSTERY TOUR

'Let's go out today,' you said. 'A day trip to the sea,
We'll take the boss and children with uncle, you and me.
We'll pack ourselves a picnic to eat on our way home'
A trip best not attempted, if only I had known.
'Now let us find a parking space, somewhere by the sea.'
We trammed for an eternity and stopped eventually.
It took us fifty minutes, to struggle lift and strain
With wheelchairs and equipment, then it began to rain.
We braved it for the morning and found somewhere to eat
And then they started moaning about their aching feet.
The oldies started grumbling and said they'd had enough
So onward to the vehicle, we packed up all our stuff.
Then the back seat drivers, chirped in they knew the way
While the children shifted restlessly and moaned about their day.
We then chugged down the motorway, at fifty miles an hour,
The lights were looking dodgy, then it drained all the power.
So finally to end our day, with the help of a nice man,
We made it safely back to port, in our clapped out family van.

J Freeborough

Memory Lane

>Where the leafy lane ends
>And a narrow road bends
>In all its magical charm,
>Where once we went
>And the hours we spent
>Down at Lower Slade Farm.

>The memory lingers
>As the oil lamp glimmers
>The kettle hisses on the hob,
>The son and his dad
>Who was there when a lad
>Discussing the very next job.

The five barred gate gone, we always walked through
Into the fields where the corn and potatoes grew,
Helped with bales of hay, fed the chicken too
Rabbits in the 'roughit' made many a stew.

Carvings on a tree, initials still good,
Christmas tree tall, near where the tractor shed stood,
Cut grass along the verges of the roads
With tractor and trailer picked up many loads.

Now on my own I reflect and gaze
How we enjoyed it, in so many ways.

As I wander down memory lane, I see
The homestead where lived generations of the family,
High on the ridge of the North Downs it stands
Looking across meadows where once were busy hands.

Frederick Coles

SECOND-HAND HEROES

They were for sale on a stall in the market
Eight discs of silver or gold.
A shame for the men that had earned them
Their story will never be told.

How grateful our wonderful nation
Felt at the end of the strife
To the men who had fought so bravely
And to those who had given their life.

They wrought those medals for valour
They were given with pomp and acclaim
The men had a 'pass bye' and dinner
To acknowledge their right to some fame.

The world then promptly forgot them
They were left to struggle and strive
They had to sell their medals
In order to stay alive.

D Adams

THE EXPLOSION

The weary bodies tired men
the shift is ending once again
the darkened cavern underneath
the look of pain beyond belief

The evening shift will wait at the top
they don their helmets as into the rock
the lift descends and underground
their manly bodies work the rounds

Cutting into hardened rocks
watching the hours on dusty clocks
listening for signs that all's not well
they carry on mining but the siren will tell

It warns of danger of gas ahead
the worried faces white in dread
a blast will be heard above the ground
but underneath there's a groaning sound

Into the night the rescuers work
watching for signs of life in the earth
the prayers were said for the dead that lay
but many a life was saved that day

Debra Becker

SOLDIER TOY

In the corner,
a small white boy,
with fearless eyes,
and a soldier toy.

But later in time,
he shall see,
life isn't like
he had dreamed it to be.

For one day,
he'll get his chance,
to be that soldier,
in a patriotic trance.

A gun is fired,
the boy's fearless eyes,
mumble the words
'The soldier's a lie.'

So fast the bullet,
that entered his chest,
so fast the bullet,
that laid him to rest.

And just one bullet,
killed that boy,
with fearless eyes,
and a soldier toy.

Sarah Horton

The Match

The crowds are loud and excited,
Their teams are ready and united,
The game gets off to a good start,
Their clever footwork is an art,
All eyes are on the football,
There's a goal, it's in the net,
For one team, the best moment yet,
The crowd gets louder still,
The score is one to nil,
It seems to be in the bag,
The other team's started to flag,
And now the game is over,
One team and their fans are in clover.

Anne R Cooper

SHARON

The inner city, greets a murky morn.
Long church spires, high-rise council flats
Asian children, scream their way to school,
Running through the heavy driving rain.
Her life, in some ways, rather like this day!
Freezing streets, fleeting, paid for love!
Seedy bars, gin and ecstasy.
Until one night she took that fatal step
And then knew that only angels fly!
No prayers then, her favourite record played.
Some tears flow beside that open grave,
One last look, then they walk away
From Sharon, who took the hookers' trade.

Paul Wilkins

TIGER, TIGER BURNING BRIGHT

Tiger, tiger burning bright,
I wonder whom set you alight,
now as you blaze from head to feet,
I wonder if I might enjoy your meat!
Though respectful of your plight,
to let you burn would not be right,
and if another I chance to meet,
he will a man-eating tiger greet,
and if he finds this a gruesome sight,
and runs off screaming in the night,
I'll blame myself for not being discreet,
but a burning tiger is such a treat.

Bill Hayles

OUR BACK DOORSTEP

He said he'd never seen anything
Quite as old as that before;
Said it might be worth a few quid.
I saw the logo stamped on the back,
And doubted him not a bit.
It seemed to please him so much so,
That I told him to take it away;
A magnanimous gesture one may think,
But really I was glad to be rid.
Before he left,
He twitched his right shoulder;
Making himself cry,
As only plastic men can;
Done by mathematical equation,
Or so I've been told;
It's something I don't understand.
Though I did ask why
He should bother with tears
When synthetic can feel no pain?
He said he hadn't meant to;
But was programmed to twitch
At the sight of a gift,
And that mine was simply just fine.
I found no heart to speak;
No way to tell this plastic man
Of all the shock I'd seen,
For etched upon that piece of rock
Was a famous actor's face;
A depiction of final dawning,
On a planet ruled by apes!

Glenn Granter

CHARLIE

Charlie, the dog, everyone loved him.
The well-known dog, loyal and embracing.

One day a young lad was playing by a canal,
When accidentally he slipped down the bank and fell.

Frantically trying to swim in icy-cold water
No one around, his cries grew fainter.

Just by luck Charlie sensed his cry
As Charlie dived in so high.

With his teeth he tugged the boy to safety
But caught in the mud he couldn't get free.

For the boy, crying, he shivered back home
But poor Charlie, where had he gone?

The locals brought flowers to the riverside
For poor Charlie who had died.

Tears fell from the owners who sadly missed him
Longing for Charlie to be loving and embracing.

When early morning, a scratching sound
At the door, poor Charlie was found.

With joy and delight, their faces so happy
Charlie's come home, ears all wet and floppy.

D Riches

SILENTLY

Silently I leave you, how I will miss your lovely face,
I don't want you to leave me and go to that better place.
Nobody has ever loved me as much as you do,
Or shown me such unconditional devotion as you,
Silently I leave you and brush away an angry tear,
How can I face the morning, knowing you won't be here.

Friends try to say the right thing but I don't want to know,
They have no idea how I feel, I can't just let you go,
I am not going back to that awful place,
As I can't look at your trusting face.
Don't forget me darling, we will meet again one day,
I sit silently thinking of you as you slip peacefully away,
I can't face anyone, I feel as though I'm lost in a fog,
How I will miss you my friend, my faithful lovely dog.

Maureen Arnold

LOVE IN THE AFTERNOON

Remember the day I phoned and asked if you would meet me
Within an hour we were kissing beneath an old oak tree
That afternoon was hot, with just a gentle summer breeze
And a soothing little shower, that filtered through the trees
It was a welcome summer rain that lovingly caressed
Our hot and sweaty bodies that gleamed with mingled sweat
Each tender stroke of your hand left behind a trembling nerve
You carefully fondled your way over every line and curve
The oak tree that we leant on was a supporter of our love
Even Mother Nature blessed us as the birds sung high above
And even though the summer sun shone brightly in the sky
Our lust was safely hidden from the eyes of passers-by
In a sudden union of flesh, our souls became entwined
In body, mind and spirit, I was yours and you were mine
A final burst of pleasure, a crescendo of pure bliss
I savoured your every touch and treasured your every last kiss
The moment of union soon ended, so too our warm summer rain
My eyes were damp with tears, as real life crashed in once again
Our stolen time was over, brought back to earth with a jerk
One kiss, then back to my husband, while you must return to your work.

Bonita Hall

THROUGH THE TREES

He rides through the trees to meet the dawn
where the air is still and the ravens sleep,
through the wooded hills and the valleys deep,
to keep a heart from being torn.

Where shrouds of mist cover the land
and tangles of briar sweep past his sight,
his faithful grey won't rest tonight,
when daybreak comes he must win her hand.

He comes to the clearing where stands his foe,
black cloak drawn up around the face,
the steam from the grey betrays the pace
of the animal's run, when the sun was low.

Sword upon sword they circle the clearing,
thrust upon thrust till the metal it rings,
heart beats so fast with the blood that it sings,
the time for winning his lady is nearing.

At the edge of the forest a figure doth tarry,
drawn like a moth to the flame of the fire,
he rode through the trees to take her heart higher,
when the fight is over, this lady he'll marry.

Her mournful cry, a sound she can't hide,
his eyes fly towards her, on her face they do rest,
the vision eludes him, what's this pain in his chest!
He stumbles towards her with his arms open wide.

She kneels down beside him kissing lips that grow slack.
In depths of despair, to her God she must pray.
Her ear to his lips as he struggles to say,
'Tell me my love, why is the sky turning black?'

John Costin

My Pet

I don't call him a pet, he is my friend
He is with me all day to watch and defend
He looks up at me with those big almond eyes
As much as to say 'It's time to exercise.'
I open the door and, nose to the ground,
He is off like a rocket without a sound.
Up the lane, over the fields,
I can't keep up but I keep my eyes peeled.
I carry on but he's out of sight.
Now I'm getting in quite a plight.
Back home I went, feet feeling sore.
Hoping and praying he was by the front door.
But sadly to say he was not there
My heart felt heavy and I cried in despair.
'What do I do next?' I thought to myself.
It's no good sitting feeling sorry for oneself.
Two days went by, not a sound.
So in the paper, in the 'Lost and found'.
Mind in a whirl, don't know which way to turn.
Hoping the phone would ring and I would learn,
That he was safe and soon to return.
Later that day the phone did ring,
A voice said 'He's well.' I just wanted to sing.
'I'll be right over and bring a lead.'
But really there was no need.
There he sat looking guilty but proud.
With a new girlfriend he had just found
Though he lead me a dance and a puzzle
He is my best friend ever, my little Jack Russell.

Sonia Bowen

TO A GRANDDAUGHTER AND HER CHILD

Emerging like a butterfly,
You came into life,
I watched you through your childhood,
Through good days and also strife.
To me you are a beauty,
Not always full of grace,
But you helped me through the bad days,
With a smile upon your face.
Now you are a chrysalis
Waiting with baited breath,
To see another butterfly appear,
To wish it happiness and good health.

Maureen Lindsey

Cats By Night

Ears pricked back, you remind me of an owl
Sitting on the window on your nightly prowl
Wide, beady eyes, staring
Looking for prey, glaring
Was that a rat you saw or a mouse
Running rampant up the wall of the house?
A bird sitting with crumbs at her table
Crow, perched high on an overhead cable
Did you hear something nocturnal hoot,
Car horn go beep or toot?
Something winged gliding in the sky
Or just someone passing by?
Perhaps another moggy,
Cloudy, Misty, Bleak or Foggy?

Ann Copland

KILLING FIELDS

The night is still, you can hear every sound,
the shrill of the shrew as it scurries around.
Barn owl perched with menacing eyes,
Cat with stealth will let nothing pass by.
One year is a lifetime for the shrew,
to live that long will be the right of some,
a chosen few.
Their life a cycle of eating and roaming,
a never-ending game of death, to stay alive
they must keep moving.
By nature they are loners, they do as they will,
Their only company, when a predator makes a kill.
The new morning dawns, all is calm,
the shrew, so active is never far from harm.

Dorrien Thomas

My Journey

I went on a journey yesterday,
And it took me far, far away.
I was in a cave wherever that may be,
And it made me open my eyes and see.
I went through a tunnel,
Which was kinda' like a funnel.
At the end of my twists and turns I came to cease,
For I found the fountain of my inner peace.
Through another tunnel my advisor stood,
His hand out open and his head covered with a hood.
In his cave he showed me my inner rebel,
It was so angry and mad and on a different level.
I told it, it was a part of me which had to go,
It showed its sadness as it hung its head low.
I said the anger and madness had to go away,
Never to come back, even on my darkest day.
It nodded its head and placed in my hand a little seed,
Of which it said I'd need.
For I had to finish my journey which was the jungle of my mind,
And it told me never to look behind.
The object was a huge knife,
Of which I had to cut down the bracken of my life.
For this was my only way out,
To find my inner peace and to what life is all about.
Then my journey stopped dead in its track,
Leaving me in doubt as to whether I'll find my way back.
To this day I still don't know,
How far on my journey I will go.
So for now I'm left in doubt,
As to whether I'll find my inner peace and to what life is all about.

J Steggles

SUBMISSIONS INVITED
SOMETHING FOR EVERYONE

POETRY NOW 2000 - Any subject, any style, any time.

WOMENSWORDS 2000 - Strictly women, have your say the female way!

STRONGWORDS 2000 - Warning! Age restriction, must be between 16-24, opinionated and have strong views. (Not for the faint-hearted)

All poems no longer than 30 lines. Always welcome! No fee! Cash Prizes to be won!

Mark your envelope (eg *Poetry Now*) **2000**
Send to:
Forward Press Ltd
Remus House, Coltsfoot Drive,
Woodston,
Peterborough, PE2 9JX

**OVER £10,000 POETRY PRIZES
TO BE WON!**

Judging will take place in October 2000